ACES
MORE RECIPES FROM THE BEST OF BRIDGE

FIFTH EFFORT
"TENTH TIME 'ROUND"

WRITTEN AND PUBLISHED BY:

THE BEST OF BRIDGE PUBLISHING LTD.
6037 - 6TH STREET S.E.
CALGARY, ALBERTA, CANADA T2H 1L8

PRINTED IN CANADA BY CENTAX BOOKS
A DIVISION OF PW GROUP

WINDING STAIR PRESS IS AN IMPRINT OF
STEWART HOUSE PUBLISHING INC.
DISTRIBUTED IN THE UNITED STATES BY
STEWART HOUSE PUBLISHING INC.
1-866-574-6873   WWW.STEWARTHOUSEPUB.COM

FOOD PHOTOGRAPHY BY SIMON CHEUNG

PORTRAIT PHOTOGRAPH BY PATRICIA HOLDEN

FIFTH EFFORT PUBLISHED SEPTEMBER, 1992

— WITH LOVE —

TO OUR PARENTS

WHO UNFAILINGLY SUPPORTED US WITH ENTHUSIASM, HUMOR, WISDOM AND GREAT LOVE. WE THANK YOU - YOU'LL ALWAYS BE "ACES" WITH US.

KAREN BRIMACOMBE	HELEN MILES
LINDA JACOBSON	VAL ROBINSON
MARY HALPEN	JOAN WILSON
MARILYN LYLE	

CANADIAN CATALOGUING IN PUBLICATION DATA
MAIN ENTRY UNDER TITLE:
ACES: MORE RECIPES FROM THE BEST OF BRIDGE

ISBN 0-9690425-5-8

1. COOKERY. 2. ENTERTAINING.
I. BEST OF BRIDGE PUBLISHING LTD.

TX714. A25 1992   641. 5   C92-098094-5

FORWARD & BACKWARD

FORWARD THINKING AND BACKWARD LOOKING ..... IS IT IN THE GREEN BOOK OR THE YELLOW BOOK, NOT THE BLACK BUT MAYBE THE RED? WELL, WHERE IS THAT RECIPE? WE'VE ALL HAD THE SAME PROBLEM AND, FINALLY, HERE'S THE SOLUTION - A COMBINED INDEX! SIXTEEN YEARS AGO WHO WOULD HAVE GUESSED THAT "MONA'S MOTHERS' MOTHERS' BEST FRIENDS' FAVORITE" WOULD BE INCLUDED IN A COMBINED INDEX OF FIVE BEST OF BRIDGE COOKBOOKS! IN CREATING THE NEW BOOK AND COMPILING THIS INDEX WE'VE REMINISCED ABOUT THE LAUGHTER AND GOOD TIMES WE'VE ENJOYED SINCE IT ALL BEGAN. MANY OF OUR MEMORIES ARE ABOUT YOU, OUR FRIENDS AND CUSTOMERS. WE THANK YOU FOR YOUR ENCOURAGEMENT; WE ARE ALWAYS GRATEFUL FOR YOUR ENTHUSIASM AND SUPPORT.

A FORK LIFT, COMPUTER AND FAX MACHINE MAY LESSEN THE LOAD BUT WE CONTINUE TO DO IT ALL OURSELVES - FROM SHIPPING TO MARKETING. EACH ONE WITH A JOB TO DO BUT ALWAYS WILLING TO FILL IN WHEN PERSONAL LIVES TAKE PRIORITY. EQUIPPED WITH THE FRIENDSHIP WE HAVE SHARED FROM THE BEGINNING, OUR SENSE OF HUMOR AND THE SATISFACTION WE HAVE IN THE ONGOING SUCCESS OF OUR BUSINESS - WE'RE BACK AGAIN WITH "ACES". OVER THE PAST YEAR OUR OFFICE HAS BECOME THE FAVORITE NEIGHBORHOOD STOP. THE POSTMAN, THE DELIVERY MAN AND THE NUTMAN CAN'T WAIT TO TASTE THE "TEST" RECIPE OF THE DAY.

OUR FOCUS CONTINUES TO BE "SIMPLE RECIPES WITH GOURMET RESULTS". WE'RE ALWAYS KEEN TO TRY NEW THINGS, LOTS OF WHICH ARE FOUND IN THIS BOOK. BUT - NOSTALGIA IS UPON US. BEFORE WE FORGET, WE'VE DECIDED TO INCLUDE SOME OF GRANDMOTHER'S FAVORITE RECIPES, OLD-FASHIONED IS UP-TO-DATE! NOR HAVE WE FORGOTTEN THE MAKE-AHEAD AND FREEZEABLES OR THE ONE-LINERS THAT KEEP YOU SMILING WHILE YOU'RE COOKING.

WE HOPE THE COMBINED INDEX PROVIDES EASY ACCESS TO ALL THE RECIPES AND THAT YOU ENJOY OUR LATEST CREATION. MAY YOUR FAMILY AND GUESTS CONTINUE TO EXCLAIM, "THAT'S ACES"!!

PICTURED ON COVER:

BEST OF BRIDGE BEAN SOUP -

PAGE 73

CHEDDAR BEER BREAD -

PAGE 25

MEDITERRANEAN PIE

IMPRESSIVE, EASY TO MAKE AND TASTES TERRIFIC!

2 SMALL ONIONS, CHOPPED	
2 GARLIC CLOVES, MINCED	
2 TBSP. BUTTER OR MARGARINE	30 mL
3 - 10 OZ. PKGS. FROZEN SPINACH, THAWED & WELL-DRAINED	3 - 283 g
2 - 14 OZ. PKGS. FROZEN PUFF PASTRY, ROLLED TO 1/8"	2 - 397 g
3/4 LB. BLACK FOREST HAM, SLICED	375 g
1 LB. MOZZARELLA CHEESE, GRATED	500 g
2 RED PEPPERS, SEEDED & DICED	
8 EGGS, BEATEN	
1 EGG, BEATEN, TO GLAZE PASTRY	

SAUTÉ ONIONS AND GARLIC IN BUTTER. STIR IN SPINACH. LINE A 10" SPRINGFORM PAN WITH PASTRY, MAKING SURE IT OVERLAPS THE SIDES. LAYER 1/2 THE HAM, 1/2 THE CHEESE, 1/2 THE RED PEPPER, 1/2 THE SPINACH MIXTURE INTO THE PIE SHELL. POUR IN 1/2 THE BEATEN EGGS. REPEAT LAYERS - PAN WILL BE FULL. COVER WITH PASTRY AND PINCH THE EDGES TO SEAL. TRIM EXCESS PASTRY AND SLASH THE TOP TO ALLOW STEAM TO ESCAPE. BRUSH TOP CRUST WITH BEATEN EGG. BAKE AT 400°F FOR 15 MINUTES, REDUCE HEAT TO 350°F AND BAKE FOR 45 MINUTES. IF THE CRUST BECOMES TOO BROWN, COVER LIGHTLY (DON'T SEAL) WITH FOIL. COOL THE PIE FOR 15 MINUTES AND REMOVE SPRING-FORM. THIS IS A SURE-FIRE HIT!
SERVES 10. (SEE PICTURE - PAGE 17.)

BREAKFAST FRUIT KABOBS

ADDS A SPECIAL TOUCH TO A BRUNCH MENU!

WATERMELON	
CANTALOUPE	
HONEYDEW	
PINEAPPLE	
STRAWBERRIES	
SEEDLESS GRAPES	
6-8 WOODEN SKEWERS	
½ CUP PLAIN YOGURT	125 mL
1 TSP. HONEY	5 mL
¼ TSP. FRESHLY GRATED NUTMEG	1 mL
2 TSP. LIME JUICE	10 mL
1 LIME, THINLY SLICED	

PREPARE FRUIT IN BALLS OR CHUNKS AND THREAD ON SKEWERS. ARRANGE ON A PLATTER. COMBINE YOGURT, HONEY, NUTMEG AND LIME JUICE. DRIZZLE OVER KABOBS. GARNISH WITH LIME SLICES.

HE WHO LAUGHS LAST IS PROBABLY THE ONE WHO INTENDED TO TELL THE STORY HIMSELF.

OLÉ! - ANOTHER WIFE-SAVER AND A GREAT MAKE AHEAD!

16 SLICES WHITE BREAD, TRIMMED		
4 LARGE, RIPE TOMATOES, SLICED		
1 MEDIUM ONION, SLICED & SEPARATED		
2 - 4 OZ. CANS CHOPPED GREEN CHILIES, DRAINED	2 - 115	g
1½ CUPS GRATED CHEDDAR OR MONTEREY JACK CHEESE	375	mL
7 EGGS		
3½ CUPS MILK	825	mL
1 TSP. SALT	5	mL
½ TSP. GARLIC SALT	2	mL
½ TSP. GROUND CUMIN	2	mL
½ TSP. CHILI POWDER	2	mL

PLACE 8 SLICES OF BREAD IN BOTTOM OF BUTTERED 9" X 13" PAN. ARRANGE TOMATO SLICES, ONION RINGS AND GREEN CHILIES OVER BREAD. SPRINKLE ⅔ OF THE CHEESE OVER ALL. TOP WITH REMAINING SLICES OF BREAD. BEAT EGGS, MILK AND SEASONINGS, POUR OVER BREAD (LIQUID SHOULD COME TO TOP OF PAN). IF MORE LIQUID IS NEEDED, ADD MIXTURE OF ONE EGG AND ½ CUP MILK. SPRINKLE REMAINING CHEESE OVER TOP. COVER WITH FOIL AND REFRIGERATE OVERNIGHT. REMOVE FROM REFRIGERATOR ONE HOUR BEFORE BAKING FOR A LIGHTER AND FLUFFIER DISH. PREHEAT OVEN TO 350°F. BAKE, UNCOVERED, FOR 1 TO 1½ HOURS OR UNTIL KNIFE

MEXICAN STRATA

THIS RECIPE CONTINUED FROM PAGE 8.

INSERTED IN CENTER COMES OUT CLEAN. ALLOW TO STAND 5 MINUTES BEFORE SERVING. SERVE WITH PICANTE SALSA (PAGE 37) OR PICALILLI ("GRAND SLAM" - PAGE 35). SERVES 8.

MY HUSBAND AND I JUST FIGURED OUT THE LONGEVITY OF OUR MARRIAGE. WE NEED ONE ANOTHER TO FINISH A SENTENCE.

CAMPTOWN BACON

DOO-DAH! DOO-DAH!

1/4 CUP DIJON MUSTARD	60 mL
1/3 CUP BROWN SUGAR	75 mL
1 LB. SLICED BACON	500 g

PREHEAT OVEN TO 325°F. COMBINE MUSTARD AND BROWN SUGAR AND BRUSH ON ONE SIDE OF BACON STRIPS. PLACE ON BROILER PAN AND BAKE FOR 15 MINUTES OR UNTIL BACON IS CRISP. WHEN SERVING AS AN APPETIZER, COOL BACON AND CUT INTO 4 OR 5 PIECES PER STRIP. MAKES ABOUT 75 PIECES.

AS A CHILD, I WAS VERY YOUNG.

STAMPEDE CASSEROLE

ROUND UP THE COWPOKES - THIS BRUNCH IS A MUST. IT'S EASY TO DO - BUT THEY'LL THINK YOU'VE FUSSED!

1½ LBS. BULK PORK SAUSAGE	750 g
3-4 OZ. CANS GREEN CHILIES, DRAINED	3 - 115 g
1 LB. CHEDDAR CHEESE, GRATED	500 g
1 LB. MONTEREY JACK CHEESE, GRATED	500 g
9 EGGS, BEATEN	
1 CUP MILK	250 mL
2 TBSP. FLOUR	30 mL
PAPRIKA	

BROWN SAUSAGE AND DRAIN WELL. SPLIT CHILIES AND REMOVE SEEDS. SAVE ⅓ OF THE CHILIES AND CUT IN THIN STRIPS. LAYER SAUSAGE WITH CHEESES AND REMAINING ⅔ OF CHILIES IN A GREASED 9" X 13" GLASS BAKING DISH. BEAT EGGS, MILK AND FLOUR TOGETHER UNTIL WELL-BLENDED. POUR OVER LAYERED MIXTURE. DECORATE TOP WITH STRIPS OF CHILIES IN A LATTICE-WORK PATTERN. SPRINKLE WITH PAPRIKA AND BAKE AT 350°F FOR 45 MINUTES. SERVES 12.

AT EVERY PARTY, THERE ARE TWO KINDS OF PEOPLE - THOSE WHO WANT TO GO HOME EARLY AND THOSE WHO DON'T. THE TROUBLE IS - THEY ARE ALMOST ALWAYS MARRIED TO EACH OTHER.

HAM AND SPINACH BAGUETTE

ANOTHER STUFF ALONG.

1 BAGUETTE, 24"	
2 CUPS PACKED FRESH SPINACH	500 mL
4 OZ. CREAM CHEESE	125 g
1/4 CUP CHOPPED FRESH DILL	60 mL
1 TBSP. MILK OR CREAM	15 mL
4 CUPS MINCED HAM, ABOUT 1 LB. (500 g)	1L
1/3 CUP CHOPPED, TOASTED PISTACHIOS	75 mL
1 TBSP. DIJON MUSTARD	15 mL
1/3 CUP MAYONNAISE	75 mL

SLICE BAGUETTE LENGTHWISE, HOLLOW OUT, LEAVING SHELL ABOUT 1/2" THICK. WRAP BREAD AND SET ASIDE. COOK SPINACH UNTIL LIMP, DRAIN WELL AND CHOP FINELY. IN FOOD PROCESSOR OR MIXER, BLEND CREAM CHEESE, DILL, MILK AND SPINACH UNTIL SPREADABLE. MIX HAM, PISTACHIOS, MUSTARD AND MAYONNAISE. SPREAD CHEESE MIXTURE ALL OVER INSIDE OF BAGUETTE. PACK HAM MIXTURE INTO BOTTOM HALF OF LOAF, MOUNDING SLIGHTLY. PUT LOAF BACK TOGETHER, WRAP TIGHTLY WITH FOIL AND REFRIGERATE FOR AT LEAST 2 HOURS OR UP TO 8 HOURS. SERVE IN 2" SLICES.

NOTE: TO TOAST PISTACHIOS, BAKE AT 350°F FOR 10 MINUTES OR UNTIL FRAGRANT. COOL BEFORE CHOPPING.

I MAY FORGET A FACE, BUT I NEVER FORGET A DRESS.

PÂTÉ EN BAGUETTE

EXECU-HIKERS REJOICE!

1 LB. FARMER, POLISH OR SUMMER SAUSAGE, CASINGS REMOVED	500 g
¼ CUP BUTTER, ROOM TEMPERATURE	60 mL
4 GREEN ONIONS, CHOPPED	
3 TBSP. SOUR CREAM	45 mL
2 TBSP. DIJON MUSTARD	30 mL
1 TBSP. LEMON JUICE	15 mL
1 TBSP. PREPARED HORSERADISH	15 mL
1 SHALLOT, CUT UP	
½ TSP. FRESHLY GROUND PEPPER	2 mL
¼ TSP. HOT PEPPER SAUCE	1 mL
¼ CUP FRESH CHOPPED PARSLEY	60 mL
½ TSP. DRIED BASIL	2 mL
1 BAGUETTE, 24"	

MUSTARD HORSERADISH SAUCE

¾ CUP MAYONNAISE	175 mL
1 HEAPING TBSP. DIJON MUSTARD	22 mL
1 TBSP. COARSE-GRAINED MUSTARD	15 mL
½ TSP. PREPARED HORSERADISH	2 mL
½ TSP. DRY MUSTARD	2 mL
½ TSP. WHITE WINE VINEGAR	2 mL
¼ TSP. HOT PEPPER SAUCE	1 mL
¼ TSP. WORCESTERSHIRE SAUCE	1 mL
FRESH PARSLEY FOR GARNISH	

FINELY CHOP SAUSAGE IN FOOD PROCESSOR. SET ASIDE IN A BOWL. ADD NEXT 11 INGREDIENTS TO PROCESSOR, ONE AT A TIME, BLENDING AFTER EACH ADDITION, THEN ADD TO MEAT MIXTURE.

PÂTÉ EN BAGUETTE

THIS RECIPE CONTINUED FROM PAGE 12.

THIS WILL HAVE A PÂTÉ-LIKE TEXTURE. REMOVE ENDS FROM BAGUETTE AND CUT BREAD INTO 6" SECTIONS. USING A SHARP BREAD KNIFE, HOLLOW OUT THE CENTER OF EACH BAGUETTE, LEAVING A ½" CRUST. PACK PÂTÉ INTO HOLLOWED BAGUETTES, WRAP TIGHTLY IN FOIL AND REFRIGERATE FOR UP TO 24 HOURS OR FREEZE.

TO MAKE SAUCE: COMBINE ALL INGREDIENTS. COVER AND CHILL OVERNIGHT.

TO SERVE: CUT BAGUETTES INTO ½" SLICES AND SERVE AT ROOM TEMPERATURE WITH SAUCE, RADISHES, GHERKINS AND OLIVES.
(SEE PICTURE - PAGE 53.)

BASHAW BISTRO SAUSAGE RING

2 LBS. BULK PORK SAUSAGE	1 kg
2 EGGS, BEATEN	
2 TBSP. CHOPPED ONION	30 mL
1 CUP DRY BREAD CRUMBS	250 mL
¼ CUP CHOPPED PARSLEY	60 mL

HEAT OVEN TO 350°F. MIX INGREDIENTS AND PACK INTO A 9" BUNDT PAN. BAKE 20 MINUTES. DRAIN. BAKE ANOTHER 20 MINUTES. DRAIN AGAIN. TURN ONTO A PLATTER AND SERVE WITH SCRAMBLED EGGS.

FRENCH TOAST RAPHAEL

PERFECT FOR YOUR PALATE.

6 CUPS WHITE BREAD, CRUSTS REMOVED CUT INTO 1" CUBES	1.5 L
6 OZ. CREAM CHEESE, CUT INTO SMALL CUBES	170 g
6 EGGS, WELL-BEATEN	
1 CUP MILK	250 mL
1/2 TSP. CINNAMON	2 mL
1/3 CUP DARK MAPLE SYRUP	75 mL

PLACE HALF THE BREAD IN A GREASED 8" X 8" PAN. DOT CHEESE ON TOP. COVER WITH REMAINING BREAD. COMBINE REMAINING INGREDIENTS AND POUR OVER ALL. COVER WITH PLASTIC WRAP AND REFRIGERATE OVERNIGHT. IN THE MORNING, REMOVE PLASTIC AND BAKE IN PREHEATED 375°F OVEN FOR 45 MINUTES. IT WILL BE PUFFY AND GOLDEN. SERVE IMMEDIATELY WITH EXTRA MAPLE SYRUP AND BACON OR BASHAW BISTRO SAUSAGE RING (PAGE 13). SERVES 6.

YOU CAN TELL A CHILD IS GROWING UP WHEN HE STOPS ASKING WHERE HE CAME FROM AND STARTS REFUSING TO TELL WHERE HE IS GOING.

CHEDDAR APPLE MUFFINS

AN AWARD WINNER!

3 CUPS FLOUR	750 mL
2/3 CUP SUGAR	150 mL
4 TSP. BAKING POWDER	20 mL
1 TSP. SALT	5 mL
1 TSP. CINNAMON	5 mL
2 CUPS GRATED CHEDDAR CHEESE	500 mL
2 EGGS	
1 CUP APPLE JUICE	250 mL
1/2 CUP BUTTER OR MARGARINE, MELTED	125 mL
2 CUPS PEELED, FINELY CHOPPED APPLES	500 mL

PREHEAT OVEN TO 375°F. COMBINE FLOUR, SUGAR, BAKING POWDER, SALT AND CINNAMON IN LARGE BOWL. MIX IN CHEESE. BEAT EGGS IN MEDIUM-SIZED BOWL. ADD APPLE JUICE; STIR IN BUTTER AND APPLE. ADD ALL AT ONCE TO FLOUR MIXTURE. STIR JUST UNTIL MOISTENED. FILL GREASED MUFFIN TINS. BAKE FOR 25-30 MINUTES. MAKES 2 DOZEN MEDIUM MUFFINS.

WE LIVE IN A WEIRD WORLD - LEMON JUICE IS MADE WITH ARTIFICIAL INGREDIENTS AND FLOOR WAX IS MADE WITH REAL LEMON JUICE!

CRANBERRY MUFFINS

2 CUPS CRANBERRIES, FRESH OR FROZEN, COARSELY CHOPPED	500 mL
1/3 CUP SUGAR	75 mL
1 TBSP. ORANGE RIND	15 mL
1/2 CUP ORANGE JUICE	125 mL
2 CUPS FLOUR	500 mL
1 TSP. BAKING POWDER	5 mL
1/2 TSP. BAKING SODA	2 mL
1/2 TSP. SALT	2 mL
1/2 CUP MARGARINE	125 mL
1 CUP SUGAR	250 mL
1 EGG	

PREHEAT OVEN TO 375°F. LIGHTLY GREASE MUFFIN TINS. COMBINE CRANBERRIES, 1/3 CUP SUGAR, ORANGE RIND AND ORANGE JUICE. SET ASIDE. MIX DRY INGREDIENTS TOGETHER. SET ASIDE. CREAM MARGARINE, ONE CUP SUGAR AND EGG IN LARGE BOWL. ADD CRANBERRY MIXTURE AND DRY INGREDIENTS. MIX UNTIL JUST BLENDED AND SPOON INTO MUFFIN TINS. BAKE FOR 20 MINUTES. MAKES 18 MEDIUM MUFFINS..

I KNOW A GOLFER WHO CHEATS SO MUCH, WHEN HE GOT A HOLE-IN-ONE, HE WROTE A ZERO ON HIS SCORE CARD.

PICTURED ON OVERLEAF

MEDITERRANEAN PIE - PAGE 6

PUMPKIN PECAN MUFFINS

1½ CUPS FLOUR	375 mL
¾ CUP BROWN SUGAR	175 mL
2 TSP. BAKING POWDER	10 mL
¼ TSP. BAKING SODA	1 mL
¼ TSP. SALT	1 mL
½ TSP. CINNAMON	2 mL
¼ TSP. EACH - ALLSPICE, GINGER, CLOVES	1 mL
1 CUP COOKED, MASHED OR CANNED PUMPKIN	250 mL
½ CUP MILK	125 mL
⅓ CUP VEGETABLE OIL	75 mL
1 EGG	
½ CUP CHOPPED DATES	125 mL
½ CUP CHOPPED PECANS	125 mL

PREHEAT OVEN TO 375°F. COMBINE DRY INGREDIENTS AND SPICES IN MEDIUM BOWL. IN A LARGE BOWL, BEAT PUMPKIN, MILK, OIL AND EGG. ADD DRY INGREDIENTS AND MIX UNTIL MOISTENED. FOLD IN DATES AND NUTS AND SPOON INTO GREASED MUFFIN TINS. BAKE ABOUT 20 MINUTES OR UNTIL TOPS ARE GOLDEN AND SPRING BACK WHEN TOUCHED. MAKES 20 MEDIUM MUFFINS.

AN OPERA IS A PLACE WHERE A GUY GETS STABBED IN THE BACK AND, INSTEAD OF BLEEDING, HE SINGS.

A PAIL FULL OF MUFFINS

AN OLD RECIPE BUT THE BEST! THE BATTER WILL KEEP IN THE REFRIGERATOR FOR UP TO 6 WEEKS - MAKES 6 DOZEN MUFFINS.

2 CUPS BOILING WATER	500 mL
2 CUPS 100% BRAN	500 mL
3 CUPS WHITE SUGAR	750 mL
1 CUP MARGARINE	250 mL
4 EGGS	
1 QT. BUTTERMILK (PLAIN YOGURT IS A GOOD SUBSTITUTE)	1 L
5 CUPS FLOUR	1.25 L
3 TBSP. BAKING SODA	45 mL
1 TBSP. SALT	15 mL
4 CUPS BRAN FLAKES	1 L
CHOPPED DATES, RAISINS OR BLUEBERRIES (OPTIONAL)	

POUR BOILING WATER OVER BRAN AND LET STAND. CREAM SUGAR AND MARGARINE. ADD EGGS TO SUGAR MIXTURE AND BEAT WELL. ADD BUTTERMILK AND BRAN MIXTURE. SIFT FLOUR, SODA, SALT AND ADD TO BRAN FLAKES. FOLD DRY INGREDIENTS INTO LIQUID MIXTURE SLOWLY UNTIL MIXED. STORE IN AIRTIGHT CONTAINER IN REFRIGERATOR, AT LEAST 24 HOURS. BEFORE BAKING, ADD DATES, RAISINS OR BLUEBERRIES. BAKE AS FEW OR AS MANY MUFFINS AS YOU WANT. SPOON INTO GREASED MUFFIN TINS. BAKE AT 400°F FOR 15-20 MINUTES.

OAT BRAN MUFFINS

1 cup flour	250 mL
1 cup oat bran	250 mL
¾ cup brown sugar	175 mL
2 tsp. baking soda	10 mL
1 tsp. baking powder	5 mL
1 tsp. nutmeg	5 mL
2 tsp. cinnamon	10 mL
½ tsp. salt	2 mL
1½ cups shredded carrots (about 4)	375 mL
2 large apples, peeled & shredded	
½ cup raisins or currants	125 mL
¼ cup vegetable oil	60 mL
½ cup skim milk	125 mL
2 eggs, slightly beaten	
1 tsp. vanilla	5 mL

Preheat oven to 375°F. Combine dry ingredients. Combine carrots, apples and raisins. Stir into dry ingredients until evenly blended. Add oil, milk, eggs and vanilla. Stir until all ingredients are just moistened. Spoon into greased muffin tins. Bake 15-18 minutes. Makes about 20 medium muffins.

What is high in fibre, low in calories and cholesterol, has no sodium and tastes great - nothing!

PIZZA MUFFINS

MAKES 12 LARGE MUFFINS TO PERK UP THOSE LUNCH BOX BLUES.

1½ CUPS CHOPPED PEPPERONI SAUSAGE	375 mL
1 GREEN PEPPER, SEEDED & FINELY CHOPPED	
10 OZ. CAN SLICED MUSHROOMS	285 g
1 MEDIUM ONION, FINELY CHOPPED	
1¼ CUPS GRATED MONTEREY JACK CHEESE	300 mL
½ CUP PIZZA SAUCE	125 mL
2 TSP. GARLIC POWDER	10 mL
½ TSP. CRUSHED CHILIES	2 mL
5 EGGS	
¼ CUP OIL	60 mL
1¼ CUPS FLOUR	300 mL
1 TBSP. BAKING POWDER	15 mL

PREHEAT OVEN TO 375°F. COMBINE FIRST 8 INGREDIENTS. IN ANOTHER BOWL, BEAT EGGS, BLEND IN OIL AND ADD FLOUR AND BAKING POWDER. BEAT UNTIL SMOOTH. STIR IN PEPPERONI MIXTURE UNTIL WELL-BLENDED. SPOON MIXTURE INTO GREASED MUFFIN TINS. BAKE FOR 20-25 MINUTES, OR UNTIL LIGHTLY BROWNED. SERVE WARM OR COLD. THESE KEEP WELL IN THE REFRIGERATOR.

SIGN IN GIFT SHOP WINDOW: UNSUPERVISED CHILDREN WILL BE TOWED AWAY.

LUNCH BOX MUFFINS

AREN'T YOU A GOOD MOM?

1½ CUPS BROCCOLI, FINELY CHOPPED	375 mL
1½ CUPS CHOPPED COOKED HAM	375 mL
1 MEDIUM ONION, CHOPPED	
½ CUP GRATED PARMESAN CHEESE	125 mL
6 EGGS	
½ CUP VEGETABLE OIL	125 mL
1¼ CUPS FLOUR	300 mL
1 TBSP. BAKING POWDER	15 mL
1 TSP. OREGANO	5 mL
1 TSP. PARSLEY	5 mL
¼ TSP. THYME	1 mL
½ TSP. GARLIC POWDER	2 mL

PREHEAT OVEN TO 375°F. COOK BROCCOLI UNTIL TENDER CRISP. IN LARGE BOWL, COMBINE BROCCOLI, HAM, ONION AND CHEESE. IN ANOTHER BOWL BEAT EGGS UNTIL FOAMY; BLEND IN OIL. ADD THE DRY INGREDIENTS; BEAT UNTIL SMOOTH. STIR IN BROCCOLI MIXTURE UNTIL JUST BLENDED. SPOON INTO GREASED MUFFIN TINS. BAKE FOR 20-25 MINUTES OR UNTIL LIGHTLY BROWNED. MAY BE SERVED WARM OR COLD. MAKES 12 LARGE MUFFINS.

IN THE OLDEN DAYS, KIDS REFUSED TO GO TO SCHOOL IF THEY HAD HOLES IN THEIR JEANS – NOW THEY REFUSE TO GO IF THEY DON'T!

SAVORY TOMATO BREAD

DELICIOUS WITH SOUP OR SALAD. TO LOOSEN TOMATO SKINS, POUR BOILING WATER OVER THEM AND LET SIT FOR 2 MINUTES.

3 CUPS FLOUR	750 mL
1 TSP. SALT	5 mL
1 TSP. BAKING SODA	5 mL
1/2 TSP. BAKING POWDER	2 mL
2 TSP. CINNAMON	10 mL
3 OR 4 MEDIUM TOMATOES	
3 EGGS	
1 1/2 CUPS SUGAR	375 mL
1 CUP VEGETABLE OIL	250 mL
1 TSP. VANILLA	5 mL

PREHEAT OVEN TO 350°F. IN A BOWL STIR TOGETHER FLOUR, SALT, BAKING SODA, BAKING POWDER AND CINNAMON. SET ASIDE. PEEL TOMATOES. CUT EACH IN HALF AND REMOVE SEEDS. FINELY CHOP TO MAKE 2 CUPS FIRM TOMATO PULP; SET ASIDE. IN A LARGE BOWL, LIGHTLY BEAT EGGS USING A WIRE WHISK. ADD SUGAR AND OIL. STIR UNTIL BLENDED. STIR IN VANILLA AND TOMATO PULP. MIX IN FLOUR MIXTURE ALL AT ONCE AND STIR JUST UNTIL EVENLY MOISTENED. POUR INTO 2 GREASED AND FLOURED 4" X 8" LOAF PANS. BAKE FOR 50-60 MINUTES. LET COOL IN PANS ON WIRE RACKS FOR AT LEAST 10 MINUTES. TURN OUT ON RACKS TO COOL COMPLETELY. (BREAD WILL BE EASIER TO SLICE IF STORED UNTIL NEXT DAY.) WRAP TIGHTLY AND REFRIGERATE. FREEZES BEAUTIFULLY.

CHEDDAR BEER BREAD

THIS ONLY TAKES 10 MINUTES TO PUT TOGETHER AND YOU WILL LOOK LIKE A PRO!

3 CUPS FLOUR	750 mL
1 TBSP. BAKING POWDER	15 mL
¾ TSP. SALT	3 mL
2 TBSP. SUGAR	30 mL
2 CUPS GRATED SHARP CHEDDAR CHEESE	500 mL
½ CUP FINELY CHOPPED ONION	125 mL
3 GARLIC CLOVES, MINCED	
12 OZ. CAN BEER	341 mL

PREHEAT OVEN TO 350°F. ALL YOU NEED IS A FORK AND A BOWL. COMBINE ALL THE INGREDIENTS (EXCEPT THE BEER) UNTIL WELL MIXED. ADD BEER A QUARTER AT A TIME UNTIL ALL THE INGREDIENTS ARE BLENDED. SPOON INTO A GREASED AND FLOURED 4" X 8" LOAF PAN (OR A SERIES OF SMALL LOAF PANS) AND SMOOTH DOWN WITH FORK. BAKE FOR ONE HOUR. REMOVE FROM PAN AND COOL ON WIRE RACK. SERVE WARM WITH SOUP OR STEW. (SEE COVER PICTURE.)

BEER MAKES YOU SMARTER - IT MADE BUDWEISER.

CINNAMON LOAF

TRY THIS TOASTED.

TOPPING

2 TBSP. CINNAMON	30	mL
1/3 CUP SUGAR	75	mL

BATTER

1/2 CUP MARGARINE	125	mL
1 CUP SUGAR	250	mL
2 EGGS		
2 CUPS FLOUR	500	mL
1 TSP. BAKING POWDER	5	mL
1/2 TSP. BAKING SODA	2	mL
1/2 TSP. SALT	2	mL
2 TSP. VANILLA	10	mL
1 CUP BUTTERMILK	250	mL

PREHEAT OVEN TO 350°F. MIX CINNAMON AND SUGAR AND SET ASIDE. CREAM MARGARINE AND SUGAR. ADD EGGS AND BEAT UNTIL BLENDED. COMBINE DRY INGREDIENTS. MIX VANILLA WITH BUTTERMILK. ADD DRY INGREDIENTS ALTERNATELY WITH MILK. POUR 1/2 THE BATTER INTO A 4" X 8" GREASED LOAF PAN. SPRINKLE WITH 1/2 THE TOPPING, STIRRING A LITTLE. ADD REMAINING BATTER AND SPRINKLE WITH REMAINING TOPPING, ONCE AGAIN STIRRING A LITTLE. BAKE FOR 50-60 MINUTES.

A CLOSED MOUTH GATHERS NO FEET.

LEMON CREAM CHEESE CRESCENTS

PASTRY

¼ CUP BUTTER OR MARGARINE, SOFTENED   60 mL
1 CUP COTTAGE CHEESE   250 mL
1 CUP FLOUR   250 mL

FILLING

4 OZ. CREAM CHEESE   115 g
¼ CUP SUGAR   60 mL
GRATED RIND OF ONE LEMON
BERRY SUGAR TO SPRINKLE

PREHEAT OVEN TO 350°F. COMBINE PASTRY INGREDIENTS UNTIL WELL-BLENDED. DIVIDE INTO 3 BALLS, COVER AND PLACE IN REFRIGERATOR WHILE MAKING THE FILLING.

TO MAKE FILLING: BLEND CREAM CHEESE, SUGAR AND LEMON RIND. ROLL ONE BALL ON LIGHTLY FLOURED BOARD INTO A 9" CIRCLE. SPREAD WITH ⅓ OF THE FILLING. CUT INTO 8 TRIANGULAR WEDGES (AS FOR A PIZZA). ROLL UP EACH WEDGE FROM THE WIDE END TOWARD CENTER AND CURVE SLIGHTLY INTO CRESCENTS. REPEAT WITH THE OTHER BALLS. SPRINKLE WITH SUGAR. CRESCENTS CAN BE ASSEMBLED TO THIS POINT AND REFRIGERATED OVERNIGHT OR FROZEN. BAKE ON A LIGHTLY GREASED COOKIE SHEET FOR 25 MINUTES. BEST SERVED WARM BUT DO NOT MICROWAVE. MAKES 24.

NEVER MISTAKE ENDURANCE FOR HOSPITALITY.

FLAKY FREEZER BISCUITS

THESE WONDERFUL BISCUITS CAN BE BAKED IMMEDIATELY OR FROZEN AND BAKED AS NEEDED.

1 PKG. YEAST (1 TBSP.)	15 mL
2 TBSP. SUGAR	30 mL
¼ CUP WARM WATER	60 mL
5 CUPS FLOUR	1.25 L
3 TBSP. SUGAR	45 mL
1 TBSP. BAKING POWDER	15 mL
1 TSP. BAKING SODA	5 mL
1 TSP. SALT	5 mL
1 CUP BUTTER OR MARGARINE	250 mL
2 CUPS BUTTERMILK	500 mL

IN A SMALL BOWL COMBINE YEAST AND SUGAR IN WATER. SET ASIDE FOR 10 MINUTES. IN A LARGE BOWL MIX FLOUR, SUGAR, BAKING POWDER, SODA AND SALT. CUT IN BUTTER TO FORM A CRUMBLY MIXTURE. STIR IN YEAST MIXTURE AND BUTTERMILK. MIX JUST ENOUGH TO HOLD DOUGH TOGETHER. ROLL DOUGH ¾" THICK ON FLOURED SURFACE. CUT OUT BISCUITS WITH THE TOP OF A GLASS OR A CUTTER. PRICK TOPS WITH FORK. FREEZE SEPARATELY ON COOKIE SHEET. AFTER BISCUITS ARE FROZEN, STACK AND WRAP WELL. BEFORE BAKING LET RISE UNTIL DOUBLED IN SIZE. BAKE AT 425°F FOR 15 MINUTES ON A LIGHTLY GREASED COOKIE SHEET. MAKES 3-4 DOZEN.

ALTERNATIVE: GRATED CHEDDAR CHEESE MAY BE ADDED TO SOFT DOUGH FOR FLAKY CHEESE BISCUITS.

"LAND OF NOD" CINNAMON BUNS

WHO WOULD THINK YOU COULD BE THIS
ORGANIZED SO EARLY IN THE A.M. !!

20 FROZEN DOUGH ROLLS		
1 CUP BROWN SUGAR	250 mL	
¼ CUP VANILLA INSTANT PUDDING	60 mL	
1-2 TBSP. CINNAMON	15-30 mL	
¾ CUP RAISINS (OPTIONAL)	175 mL	
¼-½ CUP MELTED BUTTER	60-125 mL	

BEFORE YOU PUT THE CAT OUT AND TURN OFF
THE LIGHTS, GREASE A 10" BUNDT PAN AND ADD
FROZEN ROLLS. SPRINKLE WITH BROWN SUGAR,
PUDDING POWDER, CINNAMON AND RAISINS. POUR
MELTED BUTTER OVER ALL. COVER WITH A CLEAN,
DAMP CLOTH. (LEAVE OUT AT ROOM TEMPERATURE)
TURN OUT THE LIGHTS AND SAY GOODNIGHT!

IN THE MORNING, PREHEAT OVEN TO 350°F AND
BAKE FOR 25 MINUTES. LET SIT FOR 5 MINUTES
AND THEN TURN OUT ON A SERVING PLATE. NOW,
AREN'T YOU CLEVER?

THE TROUBLE WITH LOSING WEIGHT IS THAT
YOU CAN FIND IT AGAIN WITHOUT EVEN
OFFERING A REWARD!

SEASONED FLATBREAD

IS THERE A CARPENTER IN THE HOUSE?

8 OZ. PKG. KAVLI THIN FLATBREAD	240 g
½ CUP BUTTER OR MARGARINE, SOFTENED	125 mL
2 LARGE GARLIC CLOVES, MINCED	
⅓ CUP GRATED PARMESAN CHEESE	75 mL
1 TBSP. FINELY CHOPPED, FRESH PARSLEY	15 mL

PREHEAT OVEN TO 325°F. USING A BREAD KNIFE, SAW STACKED FLATBREAD IN HALVES OR THIRDS. COMBINE BUTTER, GARLIC, CHEESE AND PARSLEY AND MIX WELL. SPREAD BUTTER MIXTURE ON FLATBREAD PIECES AND PLACE ON COOKIE SHEET. BAKE FOR ABOUT 5 MINUTES. LET COOL AND STORE IN COVERED CONTAINER OR FREEZE.

CHILI CHEESE BREAD

MAKE THIS ONCE - AND YOU'RE HOOKED!

3 CUPS GRATED MONTEREY JACK CHEESE	750 mL
4 OZ. CAN DICED GREEN CHILIES, DRAINED	115 g
1 CUP MAYONNAISE	250 mL
1 LOAF FRENCH BREAD	

COMBINE CHEESE, CHILIES AND MAYONNAISE. CUT BREAD INTO THICK SLICES AND SPREAD WITH CHEESE MIXTURE. PLACE ON COOKIE SHEET AND BROIL UNTIL CHEESE IS BUBBLY AND LIGHTLY BROWNED.

BRUSCHETTA

USE FIRM, RIPE, RED ROMA TOMATOES

2 LARGE GARLIC CLOVES, CHOPPED
SALT & PEPPER TO TASTE
1/3 CUP OLIVE OIL   75 mL
6-8 ROMA TOMATOES, COARSELY CHOPPED
CHOPPED FRESH BASIL OR
        1½ TBSP. (22 mL) DRIED BASIL
1 BAGUETTE, 24"
GRATED PROVOLONE, FONTINA OR
        MOZZARELLA CHEESE (OPTIONAL)

IN A SHALLOW BOWL, COMBINE GARLIC, SALT, PEPPER AND A FEW DROPS OF OIL. MASH WITH THE BACK OF A WOODEN SPOON TO MAKE A PASTE. STIR IN OLIVE OIL. ADD TOMATOES AND BASIL. TOSS GENTLY AND SET ASIDE. CUT BREAD IN HALF, LENGTHWISE. BRUSH EACH HALF WITH ADDITIONAL OIL AND PLACE UNDER A PREHEATED BROILER UNTIL GOLDEN BROWN. SPOON TOMATOES ONTO EACH HALF AND DRIZZLE WITH REMAINING OIL. (IF DESIRED, SPRINKLE WITH GRATED CHEESE.) BROIL - WATCH CAREFULLY! CUT AND SERVE IMMEDIATELY.

THE MAN WHO SAYS "I MAY BE WRONG" IS ABOUT TO GIVE YOU CONCLUSIVE EVIDENCE THAT HE ISN'T.

EMPANADAS

A SPICY, SPANISH TURNOVER.

FILLING

2 LBS. GROUND BEEF	1 kg
1 LARGE ONION, FINELY CHOPPED	
4 GARLIC CLOVES, FINELY CHOPPED	
2 TSP. CINNAMON	10 mL
½ TSP. EACH - CUMIN, CORIANDER, GROUND CLOVES	2 mL
1 TBSP. CHILI POWDER	15 mL
3 TBSP. BROWN SUGAR	45 mL
1 TBSP. VINEGAR	15 mL
½ TSP. SALT	2 mL
1 TSP. CRUSHED CHILIES	5 mL
½ CUP CHILI SAUCE	125 mL
GROUND PEPPER TO TASTE	

PASTRY

USE FROZEN PASTRY AND FOLLOW DIRECTIONS ON PACKAGE (OR MAKE FAIL PROOF PASTRY - "WINNERS" - PAGE 200). REFRIGERATE PASTRY.

TO MAKE FILLING: CRUMBLE GROUND BEEF IN SKILLET. ADD ONION AND GARLIC AND SAUTÉ UNTIL THE MEAT IS NO LONGER PINK AND ONION IS OPAQUE. DRAIN OFF EXCESS FAT. STIR IN REMAINING INGREDIENTS AND COOK 15 MINUTES OVER MEDIUM HEAT. COOL COMPLETELY.

TO MAKE TURNOVERS: PREHEAT OVEN TO 400°F. DIVIDE PASTRY INTO PIE-SIZED PORTIONS, ROLL ON A LIGHTLY FLOURED SURFACE TO ⅛" THICKNESS AND CUT OUT 3" ROUNDS.

EMPANADAS

THIS RECIPE CONTINUED FROM PAGE 32.

PLACE A SPOONFUL OF FILLING ON EACH ROUND AND FOLD PASTRY OVER. DIP FORK IN COLD WATER AND PRESS EDGES TOGETHER. PRICK TOP OF EACH TURNOVER WITH FORK. PLACE ON UNGREASED COOKIE SHEET ONE INCH APART AND BAKE FOR 20 MINUTES. THESE CAN BE FROZEN. SERVE WARM WITH SOUR CREAM, CHUTNEY OR SALSA. MAKES 4 DOZEN.

BRIE WITH SUN-DRIED TOMATOES

4 OZ. SUN-DRIED TOMATOES IN OIL, FINELY CHOPPED	115 g
3-4 GARLIC CLOVES, MINCED	
6 OZ. BRIE CHEESE	170 g
2 TBSP. CHOPPED FRESH PARSLEY	30 mL

MIX TOMATOES AND GARLIC AND PILE GENEROUSLY ON CHEESE. SPRINKLE WITH PARSLEY. (IT'S NOT NECESSARY TO REMOVE RIND FROM CHEESE.) HEAT IN OVEN AT 350°F FOR A FEW MINUTES UNTIL CHEESE IS SOFT. SERVE WITH BAGEL CHIPS OR CRACKERS.

ETERNITY - TWO PEOPLE AND A TURKEY.

PEACHY CHEESE DIP

8 OZ. CREAM CHEESE	250 g
8 OZ. PKG. IMPERIAL CHEESE (OR COLD PACK SHARP CHEDDAR)	250 g
2 TBSP. SHERRY	30 mL
1 TSP. CURRY	5 mL
3/4 CUP PEACH JAM	175 mL
PEACH CHUTNEY	
CHIVES	

USING A FOOD PROCESSOR OR ELECTRIC MIXER, BLEND CHEESES TOGETHER. ADD SHERRY, CURRY AND JAM MIXING UNTIL SMOOTH. POUR INTO STERILIZED JARS AND KEEP REFRIGERATED. TO SERVE, GARNISH WITH CHUTNEY AND CHIVES AND SET OUT WITH CRACKERS. MAKES ABOUT 2 - 8 OZ. JARS.

BRANDY CHEESE SPREAD

THE LONGER STORED - THE BETTER TASTING!

1/2 CUP BUTTER, SOFTENED	125 mL
3 CUPS GRATED CHEDDAR CHEESE	750 mL
1 TBSP. SESAME SEEDS	15 mL
2 TBSP. BRANDY	30 mL

BLEND TOGETHER, COVER AND REFRIGERATE UNTIL 1/2 HOUR BEFORE SERVING. YUMMY ON CRACKERS! MAKES 2 CUPS.

PICTURED ON OVERLEAF

STACKED PIZZA - PAGE 43

PICANTE SALSA

This is a medium hair raiser - add more hot stuff to suit your taste.

1 large onion, chopped
2 green peppers, chopped
3-4 garlic cloves, minced
3-4 fresh jalapeño peppers,
    chopped (remove seeds
    from all but one)

28 oz. can tomatoes, chopped	796 mL
14 oz. can tomato sauce	398 mL
1 tsp. oregano	5 mL
1-2 tsp. cumin	5-10 mL
1 tsp. olive oil	5 mL
1 tbsp. red wine vinegar	15 mL
½ tsp. freshly ground pepper	2 mL
1 tsp. salt	5 mL
2 dashes cayenne pepper	

Chop each of the vegetables, by hand or food processor, to desired size. Combine all ingredients in medium-sized saucepan and bring to boil. Reduce heat and simmer for 30 minutes. Pour into jars and store in the refrigerator. This can be served with absolutely everything! Makes 8 cups.

Chewing gum proves that you can have motion without progress.

PASADENA PINWHEELS

FAST 'N' EASY!

8 OZ. PKG. CREAM CHEESE	250 g
2 TBSP. MAYONNAISE	30 mL
4 OZ. CAN DICED GREEN CHILIES, DRAINED	114 mL
1 LARGE TOMATO, SEEDED & CHOPPED	
1/4 CUP FINELY CHOPPED ONION	60 mL
1 LARGE GARLIC CLOVE, MINCED	
1 TSP. CHILI POWDER	5 mL
1/2 TSP. SALT	2 mL

FLOUR TORTILLAS

BLEND CREAM CHEESE AND MAYONNAISE. STIR IN REMAINING INGREDIENTS. COVER AND REFRIGERATE FOR 2 HOURS. SPREAD CHEESE MIXTURE OVER EACH TORTILLA AND ROLL UP TIGHTLY. TRIM ENDS. REFRIGERATE UNTIL FIRM. SLICE AND PLACE PINWHEELS FLAT ON COOKIE SHEET. BROIL UNTIL LIGHTLY GOLDEN.

ALSO A TASTY DIP TO SERVE WITH TACO OR CORN CHIPS.

NOW THAT SCIENCE HAS PERFECTED THE SELF-CLEANING OVEN, WHEN ARE THEY GOING TO CREATE THE SELF-CLEANING GARAGE?

CHINESE PORK APPETIZER

1½ LBS. PORK TENDERLOIN	750 g

MARINADE

⅓ CUP SOY SAUCE	75 mL
4 TSP. DRY SAKE OR SHERRY	20 mL
2 TBSP. HONEY	30 mL
1 TSP. MINCED FRESH GINGER	5 mL
1 GARLIC CLOVE, MINCED	

SAUCE

3 TBSP. DRY MUSTARD	45 mL
1-2 TBSP. SAKE OR WATER (SAUCE SHOULD BE THIN)	15-30 mL

COMBINE MARINADE INGREDIENTS. PRICK PORK ALL OVER WITH A FORK. PLACE MEAT AND MARINADE IN ZIP-LOCK BAG. REFRIGERATE FOR 24 HOURS, TURNING OCCASIONALLY. PREHEAT OVEN TO 325°F. COVER PORK LIGHTLY WITH FOIL AND BAKE ON RACK IN PAN FOR 20 MINUTES. BRUSH WITH MARINADE AND BAKE UNCOVERED 20-30 MINUTES MORE. MEAT SHOULD NOT BE PINK. COOL AND SLICE THINLY.

COMBINE DRY MUSTARD AND SAKE OR WATER. ARRANGE MEAT ON A PLATE WITH A BOWL OF THE MUSTARD SAUCE. DIP MEAT SPARINGLY INTO SAUCE AS IT'S HOT, HOT, HOT!

SZECHUAN SESAME CHICKEN WINGS

HAVE YOU EVER MADE ENOUGH?

36 CHICKEN WINGS		
2 GARLIC CLOVES, MINCED		
1" PIECE FRESH GINGER, PEELED	2.5 cm	
2 TSP. HOT RED PEPPER FLAKES	10 mL	
2 TSP. CORIANDER	10 mL	
3 TBSP. SOY SAUCE	45 mL	
3 TBSP. LEMON JUICE	45 mL	
2 TBSP. SESAME OIL	30 mL	
2 TBSP. SUGAR	30 mL	
½ CUP SESAME SEEDS	125 mL	

REMOVE TIPS AND CUT WINGS IN HALF. PLACE CHICKEN IN SHALLOW CASSEROLE. BLEND REMAINING INGREDIENTS, EXCEPT SESAME SEEDS. POUR OVER CHICKEN, COVER AND MARINATE FOR SEVERAL HOURS. PREHEAT OVEN TO 375°F. PLACE CHICKEN ON COOKIE SHEET AND SPRINKLE WITH SESAME SEEDS. BAKE FOR 30 MINUTES.

MEMORY IS A WONDERFUL THING, IT ENABLES YOU TO REMEMBER A MISTAKE EACH TIME YOU REPEAT IT.

SPINACH BITES

KEEP A SUPPLY IN YOUR FREEZER FOR UNEXPECTED COMPANY!

¼ CUP BUTTER	60 mL
3 EGGS	
1 CUP FLOUR	250 mL
1 TSP. SALT	5 mL
1 TSP. BAKING POWDER	5 mL
1 TBSP. DIJON MUSTARD	15 mL
DASH CAYENNE PEPPER	
¼ CUP CHOPPED GREEN ONION	60 mL
1 LB. EDAM CHEESE, GRATED	500 g
2 - 12 OZ. PKGS. FROZEN CHOPPED SPINACH, THAWED & DRAINED WELL	2 - 350 g

PREHEAT OVEN TO 350°F. IN A 9" X 13" PAN, MELT BUTTER IN OVEN. IN A LARGE MIXING BOWL, BEAT EGGS AND ADD EVERYTHING BUT THE CHEESE AND SPINACH. BLEND WELL. FOLD IN CHEESE AND SPINACH. POUR OVER MELTED BUTTER. BAKE 30-35 MINUTES, OR UNTIL ALMOST SET IN CENTER. REMOVE FROM OVEN AND ALLOW TO SET FOR 10 MINUTES. CUT INTO BITE-SIZED SQUARES. YOU MAY FREEZE THESE AFTER BAKING. REHEAT IN A 350°F OVEN FOR APPROXIMATELY 15 MINUTES. SERVE WARM.

MAN IS THE ONLY ANIMAL THAT PLANTS GRASS IN THE SPRING, THEN FIGHTS ITS GROWTH ALL SUMMER.

PEPPER JELLY TURNOVERS

1 CUP VELVEETA CHEESE, SOFTENED & CUT IN CHUNKS	250 mL
½ CUP BUTTER	125 mL
1 CUP FLOUR	250 mL
PINCH OF SALT	
4 OZ. JAR HOT PEPPER JELLY ("WINNERS" - PAGE 55)	115 mL

CREAM CHEESE AND BUTTER UNTIL SMOOTH. ADD FLOUR AND SALT AND MIX TO FORM A BALL. CHILL IN REFRIGERATOR FOR 15 MINUTES. ROLL DOUGH BETWEEN LAYERS OF WAXED PAPER TO ⅛" THICKNESS. CUT CIRCLES WITH TOP OF 2" GLASS OR CUTTER. PLACE ABOUT ONE TSP. OF JELLY IN CENTER AND FOLD OVER. CRIMP EDGES WITH A FORK TO SEAL. BAKE AT 400°F FOR 10-12 MINUTES UNTIL LIGHTLY BROWNED. TURNOVERS CAN BE FROZEN BEFORE OR AFTER BAKING. REHEAT AT 250°F OR SERVE COLD. THIS RECIPE DOUBLES WELL. CRAB APPLE JELLY MAY ALSO BE USED FOR FILLING. MAKES 18.

IF YOU THINK EVERYTHING NOWADAYS IS COIN OPERATED, ASK YOUR TEENAGER TO SHOVEL SNOW FOR A QUARTER.

STACKED PIZZA

FOR ADULTS ONLY.

7 SHEETS PHYLLO PASTRY	
½ CUP BUTTER, MELTED	125 mL
7 TBSP. FRESHLY GRATED PARMESAN CHEESE	105 mL
1½ CUPS GRATED MOZZARELLA CHEESE	375 mL
1 ONION, THINLY SLICED	
5-6 ROMA TOMATOES, SLICED	
1 TSP. OREGANO	5 mL
SALT & PEPPER TO TASTE	
FRESH HERB SPRIGS - THYME, OREGANO, ROSEMARY	

PREHEAT OVEN TO 375°F. TO THAW AND PREPARE PHYLLO, FOLLOW PACKAGE INSTRUCTIONS. PLACE FIRST SHEET OF PHYLLO ON BAKING SHEET, BRUSH WITH BUTTER AND SPRINKLE WITH ONE TBSP. PARMESAN CHEESE. REPEAT UNTIL ALL SHEETS ARE USED. PRESS FIRMLY SO LAYERS WILL STICK TOGETHER. SPRINKLE TOP SHEET WITH MOZZARELLA AND ONIONS. ARRANGE TOMATO SLICES ON TOP. SEASON WITH OREGANO, SALT AND PEPPER. BAKE FOR 20-25 MINUTES, UNTIL EDGES ARE GOLDEN. DECORATE WITH HERBS AND CUT INTO SQUARES.

NOTE: OLIVES, ANCHOVIES, PEPPERS CAN ALSO BE USED - BUT DON'T OVERLOAD AS THIS IS A DELICATE CRUST! (SEE PICTURE - PAGE 35.)

TO EXERCISE IS HUMAN- NOT TO IS DIVINE!

BAKED GARLIC STARTER

BAKED GARLIC IS IN!!

GARLIC - USE 1 BULB FOR EACH PERSON (JUMBO
        OR LARGE BUT NOT ELEPHANT GARLIC)
OLIVE OIL
BRIE CHEESE
BAGUETTE, SLICED AND TOASTED.

PREHEAT OVEN TO 325°F. REMOVE ANY OF THE
LOOSE, PAPER-LIKE SKIN AND LIGHTLY BASTE
BULBS OF GARLIC WITH OLIVE OIL. WRAP IN FOIL
AND POKE A FEW HOLES TO ALLOW STEAM TO
ESCAPE. BAKE FOR 1¼ HOURS. CUT GARLIC IN
HALF HORIZONTALLY. TO SERVE, WARM BRIE IN
325°F OVEN UNTIL JUST STARTING TO MELT.
SPREAD CHEESE ON BREAD SLICES AND THEN
SPREAD WARM GARLIC PULP ON TOP.

PEOPLE WHO ARE SMART, INDUSTRIOUS, KIND,
HONEST AND LIKEABLE JUST SEEM TO HAVE ALL
THE LUCK.

PESTO CHEESE BUNDLES

ATTENTION ALL PHYLLO FIDDLERS!

1 CUP GRATED MOZZARELLA CHEESE	250 mL
3 TBSP. PESTO SAUCE	45 mL
4 PHYLLO PASTRY SHEETS	
1 EGG, BEATEN	

MIX CHEESE AND PESTO SAUCE TOGETHER. FOLLOW DIRECTIONS ON THE FROZEN PHYLLO PASTRY PACKAGE. CUT EACH PHYLLO SHEET INTO 3" SQUARES. LAY ONE SQUARE AT AN ANGLE OVER ANOTHER SQUARE (THE RESULT SHOULD BE AN 8-POINTED STAR). USING A TEASPOON, PLACE A SMALL AMOUNT OF THE CHEESE AND PESTO MIXTURE ONTO THE CENTER OF EACH SQUARE. BRUSH THE 8 CORNERS WITH EGG. GATHER CORNERS TOGETHER AND TWIST TO MAKE A BUNDLE. PLACE ON A COOKIE SHEET AND BAKE AT 350°F FOR 5 MINUTES. FREEZES WELL. TO REHEAT, PLACE ON COOKIE SHEET AND WARM IN OVEN. MAKES ABOUT 20.

THE CHEAPEST AND QUICKEST WAY TO TRACE YOUR FAMILY TREE IS TO RUN FOR PUBLIC OFFICE.

CHEESE QUESADILLAS

MEX TO THE MAX!

2 CUPS GRATED MONTEREY JACK CHEESE   500 mL

6 - 8" FLOUR TORTILLAS

4 OZ. CAN DICED GREEN CHILI PEPPERS,   114 mL
     DRAINED

SLICED, PITTED RIPE OLIVES

SALSA

AVOCADO DIP ("BEST OF BRIDGE" - PAGE 64)

SOUR CREAM

SPRINKLE ⅓ CUP CHEESE ON HALF OF EACH TORTILLA. TOP WITH PEPPERS. FOLD TORTILLA IN HALF AND GENTLY PRESS DOWN EDGES. COOK IN A LIGHTLY OILED PAN OVER MEDIUM HEAT FOR ABOUT 4 MINUTES OR UNTIL CHEESE MELTS, TURNING ONCE. CUT TORTILLAS INTO 3 TRIANGLES. KEEP WARM. SERVE WITH OLIVES, SALSA, AVOCADO DIP AND SOUR CREAM.

IF YOU AREN'T CONTENT WITH WHAT YOU HAVE, BE THANKFUL FOR WHAT YOU'VE ESCAPED.

ASPARAGUS ROLL-UPS

A GREAT APPETIZER TO MAKE AHEAD AND FREEZE.

2 WHITE SANDWICH LOAVES	
8 OZ. ROQUEFORT CHEESE	250 g
8 OZ. CREAM CHEESE	250 g
1 TBSP. MAYONNAISE	15 mL
1 EGG	
36 FRESH ASPARAGUS SPEARS	
1/2 CUP BUTTER, MELTED	125 mL

PREHEAT OVEN TO 350°F. CUT CRUSTS OFF BREAD AND ROLL EACH SLICE FLAT WITH A ROLLING PIN. COMBINE CHEESES, MAYONNAISE AND EGG IN BLENDER AND SPREAD ON BREAD. TOP WITH ONE ASPARAGUS SPEAR AND ROLL UP. CUT INTO 3 PIECES. ROLL IN MELTED BUTTER AND PLACE ON UNGREASED COOKIE SHEET. (AT THIS POINT YOU MAY LAYER ROLLS BETWEEN WAXED PAPER AND PLACE IN AN AIRTIGHT CONTAINER AND FREEZE.) BAKE FOR ABOUT 15 MINUTES OR UNTIL WELL BROWNED.

MAKES APPROXIMATELY 9 DOZEN.

THERE'S NO PLEASURE IN HAVING NOTHING TO DO - THE FUN IS HAVING LOTS TO DO AND NOT DOING ANY OF IT!

PETITE PASTIES

WHAT A FIND - YOU CAN FREEZE THESE TASTY LITTLE DEVILS FOR UP TO 3 MONTHS!

1 LB. LEAN GROUND BEEF	500 g
1 MEDIUM ONION, FINELY CHOPPED	
2 TBSP. TOMATO PASTE	30 mL
JUICE OF 1 LEMON (3 TBSP.)	45 mL
8 OZ. SOUR CREAM	250 mL
½ TSP. CINNAMON	2 mL
SALT & PEPPER TO TASTE	
2 - 10 OZ. PKGS. REFRIGERATOR BISCUITS	2 - 284 g
OIL FOR FRYING	

IN A SKILLET, BROWN MEAT AND ONION, BREAKING UP MEAT WHILE BROWNING. ADD TOMATO PASTE, LEMON JUICE, SOUR CREAM, CINNAMON, SALT AND PEPPER. STIR TOGETHER AND COOL IN REFRIGERATOR. PULL APART FREEZER BISCUITS TO MAKE 2 HALVES. ROLL EACH ON FLOURED BOARD. PLACE A HEAPING TEASPOON OF COLD FILLING ON EACH BISCUIT ROUND. FOLD OVER AND CRIMP EDGES TO SEAL. PLACE ON A TRAY AND FREEZE. WHEN FROZEN, FRY IN SMALL AMOUNT OF OIL UNTIL GOLDEN BROWN ON BOTH SIDES. DRAIN AND SERVE WARM. MAKES 40.

I WAS SO SURPRISED AT MY BIRTH, I COULDN'T TALK FOR A YEAR AND A HALF.

CAVIAR MOUSSE

CHAMPAGNE WISHES AND ? ? ?

6 EGGS, HARD-BOILED, CHOPPED	
½ MEDIUM YELLOW ONION, GRATED	
1 TBSP. WORCESTERSHIRE SAUCE	15 mL
DASH TABASCO	
¾ CUP MAYONNAISE	175 mL
1 ENVELOPE GELATIN, DISSOLVED IN	
2 TBSP. (30 mL) COLD WATER	
2 TBSP. LEMON JUICE	30 mL
3½ OZ. JAR LUMPFISH CAVIAR	100 g

COMBINE ALL INGREDIENTS EXCEPT CAVIAR. GENTLY FOLD IN CAVIAR AND POUR INTO LIGHTLY GREASED MEDIUM-SIZED MOLD. COVER AND LET STAND AT LEAST ONE DAY IN REFRIGERATOR. SERVE WITH CRACKERS.

EGGNOG SALAD MOLD

A CHRISTMAS-TIME FAVORITE!

10 OZ. CAN MANDARIN ORANGES	284 mL
3 OZ. PKG. LEMON JELLO POWDER	85 g
1-2 TSP. BRANDY OR RUM	5-10 mL
¾ CUP EGGNOG	175 mL

DRAIN ORANGES, RESERVING JUICE. ADD WATER TO JUICE TO MAKE 1¼ CUPS LIQUID. HEAT TO BOILING AND DISSOLVE JELLO POWDER. ADD BRANDY OR RUM AND EGGNOG. CHILL UNTIL SLIGHTLY THICK. FOLD IN ORANGE SECTIONS AND PUT INTO A 3-CUP MOLD. CHILL UNTIL FIRM. DECORATE WITH A SPRIG OF HOLLY.

PEAR AND WALNUT SALAD

A FINE PEAR WITH HOT NUTS

DRESSING

1 CUP OLIVE OIL	250 mL
1/4 CUP RED WINE VINEGAR	60 mL
2 TBSP. DIJON MUSTARD	30 mL
2 TSP. SUGAR	10 mL
3 GARLIC CLOVES	
SALT & PEPPER TO TASTE	

SALAD

2 TBSP. OIL - WALNUT OIL IS BEST	30 mL
1/2 CUP WALNUT PIECES	125 mL
2 LARGE FIRM PEARS	
MIXED SALAD GREENS, BOSTON OR LEAF	
LETTUCE, ENDIVE, WATERCRESS	

MIX ALL DRESSING INGREDIENTS IN BLENDER. MAKE AHEAD AND STORE IN REFRIGERATOR. HEAT 2 TBSP. OIL IN FRYING PAN. ADD WALNUTS AND SAUTÉ APPROXIMATELY 5 MINUTES UNTIL GOLDEN. SET ASIDE. PEEL, HALVE AND CUT PEARS INTO 1/4" SLICES. PLACE IN SHALLOW BOWL, COVER WITH DRESSING. LET STAND UNTIL READY TO SERVE. REMOVE PEARS. PREPARE GREENS, TOSS WITH DRESSING. SERVE AS INDIVIDUAL SALADS, ARRANGING PEARS AND NUTS ON TOP. SERVES 6-8.

IF LIFE WERE FAIR - THERE'D BE NO NEED FOR SALADS.

PAPAYA AVOCADO SALAD

1 HEAD OF ROMAINE LETTUCE
1 RIPE PAPAYA (PAPAYAS ARE RIPE
    WHEN THEY HAVE TURNED YELLOW)
1 LARGE AVOCADO, PEELED & SLICED
RED ONION SLICES

DRESSING

¼-½ CUP SUGAR	60-125 mL
½ TSP. DRY MUSTARD	2 mL
2 TSP. SALT	10 mL
2 TBSP. PAPAYA SEEDS	30 mL
½ CUP WHITE WINE VINEGAR OR	125 mL
TARRAGON VINEGAR	
½ CUP SALAD OIL	125 mL
2 GREEN ONIONS, FINELY CHOPPED	

WASH AND DRY LETTUCE. TEAR INTO BITE-SIZED
PIECES AND PLACE IN SALAD BOWL. HALVE AND
PEEL PAPAYA. SCOOP OUT SEEDS AND SAVE
2 TBSP. SLICE PAPAYA. COMBINE DRESSING
INGREDIENTS IN A BLENDER UNTIL PAPAYA
SEEDS HAVE THE APPEARANCE OF GROUND
PEPPER. STORE DRESSING IN REFRIGERATOR.
JUST BEFORE SERVING ADD PAPAYA, AVOCADO AND
RED ONION SLICES TO LETTUCE. POUR DRESSING
OVER SALAD AND TOSS. (YOU MIGHT HAVE SOME
DRESSING LEFT OVER, BUT YOU'RE GOING TO
WANT TO MAKE THIS SALAD AGAIN - SOON!)
SERVES 6-8.

THE OLDER YOU GET, THE BETTER YOU WERE.

DOUBLE GREEN SALAD

1 HEAD ROMAINE LETTUCE	
1 ENGLISH CUCUMBER	
1 CUP SEEDLESS GREEN GRAPES	250 mL
2 TBSP. CHOPPED FRESH DILL	30 mL
1/3 CUP OIL	75 mL
2 TBSP. LEMON JUICE	30 mL
3/4 TSP. SALT	3 mL
1/2 TSP. FRESHLY GROUND PEPPER	2 mL

TEAR ROMAINE INTO BITE-SIZED PIECES. SLICE CUCUMBER AND HALVE GRAPES. COMBINE AND TOSS WITH DILL. COVER TIGHTLY AND REFRIGERATE UNTIL READY TO SERVE. IN BLENDER, COMBINE REMAINING INGREDIENTS FOR DRESSING AND ADD JUST BEFORE SERVING. TOSS GENTLY. SERVE WITH WILD WEST SALMON (PAGE 125). YAHOO!

YOGURT CURRY DRESSING

SERVE ON FRESH FRUIT SALAD.

1 1/2 TSP. CURRY POWDER	7 mL
2 TBSP. CHICKEN BROTH	30 mL
1/4 CUP MAYONNAISE (LOW-FAT IS FINE)	60 mL
1/4 CUP PLAIN LOW-FAT YOGURT	60 mL
1 TSP. CHOPPED FRESH GINGER	5 mL
1 GARLIC CLOVE, MINCED	
PINCH CAYENNE PEPPER	

BLEND WELL AND REFRIGERATE.

PICTURED ON OVERLEAF

RED PEPPER SOUP - PAGE 68

PÂTÉ EN BAGUETTE - PAGE 12

BROCCOLI MANDARIN SALAD - PAGE 57

OVEN-FRIED CHICKEN - PAGE 117

SPINACH AND STRAWBERRY SALAD

SPINACH - ENOUGH FOR YOUR CREW
STRAWBERRIES - SAME AS ABOVE!

DRESSING

⅓ CUP WHITE SUGAR	75 mL
½ CUP OIL	125 mL
¼ CUP WHITE VINEGAR	60 mL
2 TBSP. SESAME SEEDS	30 mL
2 TBSP. POPPY SEEDS	30 mL
¼ TSP. PAPRIKA	1 mL
½ TSP. WORCESTERSHIRE SAUCE	2 mL
1½ TSP. MINCED ONION	7 mL

TEAR SPINACH INTO BITE-SIZED PIECES. CUT
STRAWBERRIES IN HALF. COMBINE DRESSING
INGREDIENTS AND MIX WELL. TOSS WITH
SPINACH AND STRAWBERRIES.

ORANGE SHERRY DRESSING

ANOTHER CHOICE FOR FRESH FRUIT SALAD.

2 TBSP. MAYONNAISE	30 mL
3 TBSP. CREAM	45 mL
1 TBSP. DRY SHERRY	15 mL
3 TBSP. ORANGE JUICE	45 mL
SALT TO TASTE	

BLEND WELL AND REFRIGERATE.

SPINACH MELON SALAD

DRESSING

¼ CUP SALAD OIL	60 mL
1 TBSP. WHITE WINE VINEGAR	15 mL
¼ TSP. SALT	1 mL
¼ TSP. CELERY SEED	1 mL
¼ TSP. DIJON MUSTARD	1 mL

SALAD

4 CUPS TORN SPINACH	1 L
2 CUPS CANTALOUPE BALLS	500 mL
1 CUP THINLY SLICED ZUCCHINI	250 mL
2-4 TBSP. CHOPPED GREEN ONIONS	30-60 mL

COMBINE DRESSING INGREDIENTS IN A JAR, COVER AND SHAKE WELL. REFRIGERATE. COMBINE SPINACH, CANTALOUPE, ZUCCHINI AND ONIONS IN A BOWL. TOSS WITH DRESSING. SERVES 6.

ONE THING'S FOR SURE - IF YOU HAD YOUR LIFE TO LIVE OVER AGAIN, YOU'D CERTAINLY NEED MORE MONEY.

BROCCOLI MANDARIN SALAD

EVEN GEORGE WILL LIKE THIS!

DRESSING

2 EGGS	
½ CUP SUGAR	125 mL
1 TSP. CORNSTARCH	5 mL
1 TSP. DRY MUSTARD	5 mL
¼ CUP WHITE WINE VINEGAR	60 mL
¼ CUP WATER	60 mL
½ CUP MAYONNAISE	125 mL

SALAD

4 CUPS FRESH BROCCOLI FLORETS	1 L
½ CUP RAISINS	125 mL
8 SLICES BACON, COOKED & CHOPPED	
2 CUPS SLICED FRESH MUSHROOMS	500 mL
½ CUP SLIVERED TOASTED ALMONDS	125 mL
10 OZ. CAN MANDARIN ORANGES, DRAINED	284 mL
½ RED ONION, SLICED	

TO MAKE DRESSING: IN A SAUCEPAN, WHISK TOGETHER EGGS, SUGAR, CORNSTARCH AND DRY MUSTARD. ADD VINEGAR AND WATER AND COOK SLOWLY UNTIL THICKENED. REMOVE FROM HEAT AND STIR IN MAYONNAISE. COOL.

TO MAKE SALAD: MARINATE BROCCOLI IN DRESSING FOR SEVERAL HOURS. ADD REMAINING INGREDIENTS AND TOSS WELL. SERVES 6. (SEE PICTURE - PAGE 53.)

YUCATÁN SALAD

A COOL AMIGO TO A SPICY MEXICAN DISH.

A VARIETY OF LETTUCE & SPINACH TO SERVE
    8 HOMBRES
1½ CUPS JICAMA, CUT INTO THIN STRIPS   375 mL
1 MEDIUM RED ONION, THINLY SLICED
1 GRAPEFRUIT, PEELED & WHITE
    MEMBRANE REMOVED
2 ORANGES, PEELED & WHITE
    MEMBRANE REMOVED
1 LARGE AVOCADO

DRESSING

2 TBSP. CIDER VINEGAR   30 mL
2 TBSP. LIME JUICE   30 mL
⅓ CUP OLIVE OIL   75 mL
1 GARLIC CLOVE
1 TSP. SALT   5 mL
1 TSP. CUMIN   5 mL
⅛ TSP. CRUSHED RED CHILI PEPPER   0.5 mL
    FLAKES

IN A LARGE SALAD BOWL, MIX GREENS AND JICAMA. ARRANGE ONION RINGS ON TOP. CUT GRAPEFRUIT AND ORANGES INTO SECTIONS AND ARRANGE OVER ONIONS. COVER AND REFRIGERATE FOR AT LEAST 2 HOURS. MIX THE DRESSING INGREDIENTS UNTIL WELL-BLENDED. JUST BEFORE SERVING, PEEL, PIT AND SLICE THE AVOCADO AND ARRANGE ON SALAD. ADD DRESSING AND TOSS GENTLY.

SALAD WITH WARM VINAIGRETTE

A GOOD WINTER SALAD - THE CRUNCHY FRIED ONIONS MAKE IT!

½ CUP OLIVE OIL	125 mL
2 MEDIUM YELLOW ONIONS, THINLY SLICED	
½ CUP PECAN HALVES	125 mL
2 TBSP. BALSAMIC VINEGAR	30 mL
5 CUPS MIXED GREENS	1.25 L

HEAT 2 TBSP. OF THE OIL IN A LARGE FRYING PAN. SAUTÉ ONIONS OVER MEDIUM HEAT UNTIL GOLDEN AND CRISP. TRANSFER TO A PLATE. ADD PECANS AND SAUTÉ FOR A FEW MINUTES. SET ASIDE. IN SAME PAN OVER LOW HEAT, ADD THE REMAINING OLIVE OIL AND VINEGAR. WHISK LIGHTLY. PLACE GREENS ON SALAD PLATES. POUR WARM DRESSING OVER AND GARNISH WITH ONIONS AND PECANS. SERVES 4.

HER GOSSIP IS SO INTERESTING YOU ALWAYS WISH YOU KNEW THE PERSON SHE IS TALKING ABOUT.

SUNSHINE SALAD

2 HEADS BUTTER LETTUCE
1 CUP CUBED MONTEREY JACK CHEESE   250 mL
3 FIRM, RIPE NECTARINES, SLICED
2 BANANAS, PEELED, SLICED
1 CUP FRESH OR CANNED PINEAPPLE CHUNKS   250 mL
    (RESERVE 1 TBSP. JUICE FOR
    DRESSING)
2 CUPS CUBED CANTALOUPE   500 mL
2 CUPS RED SEEDLESS GRAPES, HALVED   500 mL
1/4 CUP BROKEN, TOASTED PECANS   60 mL

DRESSING

1/2 CUP SALAD OIL   125 mL
1/4 CUP FROZEN ORANGE JUICE   60 mL
    CONCENTRATE, THAWED
2 TBSP. HONEY   30 mL
1/2 TSP. SALT   2 mL
1/2 TSP. GROUND GINGER   2 mL
1 TBSP. PINEAPPLE JUICE   15 mL

TEAR LETTUCE INTO BITE-SIZED PIECES.
COMBINE ALL SALAD INGREDIENTS EXCEPT
PECANS. PLACE IN GLASS BOWL. BLEND DRESSING
INGREDIENTS, BEATING WELL. JUST BEFORE
SERVING, POUR DRESSING OVER SALAD AND TOSS.
TOP WITH PECANS. SERVES 6.

WHY DO THE MOTHERS ON SOAP OPERAS LOOK
ONLY A YEAR OLDER THAN THEIR DAUGHTERS?

CHICKEN AND ASPARAGUS SALAD

4 CUPS COOKED & CUBED CHICKEN	1 L
1 LB. ASPARAGUS, COOKED & CUT IN 1" PIECES	500 g
1 CUP CHOPPED CELERY	250 mL
1 CUP WALNUTS OR SLIVERED TOASTED ALMONDS	250 mL
½ CUP CHOPPED GREEN ONIONS	125 mL
1 CUP LIGHT MAYONNAISE	250 mL
¼ CUP LIGHT SOUR CREAM	60 mL
2 TBSP. LEMON JUICE	30 mL
1 TBSP. DIJON MUSTARD	15 mL
½ TSP. HOT PEPPER SAUCE	2 mL
SALT & PEPPER TO TASTE	

IN A GLASS BOWL, TOSS CHICKEN, ASPARAGUS, CELERY, NUTS AND GREEN ONIONS. IN SEPARATE BOWL, MIX REMAINING INGREDIENTS. POUR DRESSING OVER CHICKEN MIXTURE AND TOSS. SERVES 5-7.

THE MEEK SHALL INHERIT THE EARTH AND THE RICH AND POWERFUL WILL FIND A BETTER PLACE.

MARINATED CHINESE NOODLES AND VEGETABLES

CONTEMPORARY CUISINE - UPBEAT & LOW CAL!
BREAK OUT THE CHOPSTICKS

MARINADE

½ CUP OIL	125 mL
½ CUP RICE VINEGAR	125 mL
¼ CUP SOY SAUCE	60 mL
1 TBSP. SUGAR	15 mL
2 TSP. DRY MUSTARD	10 mL
1 TBSP. PEANUT BUTTER	15 mL
1 TBSP. SESAME OIL	15 mL
1 TSP. GROUND GINGER OR 1 TBSP. GRATED FRESH GINGER	5 mL

SALAD

8 OZ. THIN ORIENTAL NOODLES	250 g
2 CUPS SLICED MUSHROOMS	500 mL
24 FRESH SNOW PEAS	
1 RED BELL PEPPER, SLICED IN STRIPS	
4 GREEN ONIONS, CUT IN STRIPS USING TOPS	
4 CARROTS, PEELED & SLICED	
1 MEDIUM JICAMA, SLICED OR SLICED WATER CHESTNUTS	
¼ CUP TOASTED SESAME SEEDS	60 mL

COMBINE MARINADE INGREDIENTS AND MIX WELL. PREPARE NOODLES AS PACKAGE DIRECTS. COMBINE NOODLES AND SALAD INGREDIENTS, EXCEPT SESAME SEEDS. POUR MARINADE OVER AND TOSS.

MARINATED CHINESE NOODLES AND VEGETABLES

THIS RECIPE CONTINUED FROM PAGE 62.

COVER AND REFRIGERATE TO ABSORB FLAVORS. SPRINKLE WITH SESAME SEEDS AND SERVE AT ROOM TEMPERATURE.

LAYERED MOZZARELLA AND TOMATO SALAD

GOOD WITH LAMB OR BEEF. AN ATTRACTIVE PLATTER FOR YOUR NEXT BUFFET.

6 LARGE TOMATOES, SLICED

2 LBS. BOCCONCINI (FRESH MOZZARELLA)   1 Kg
    CUT INTO 1/4" SLICES

1/4 CUP CHOPPED FRESH BASIL   60 mL

1/4 CUP CHOPPED FRESH PARSLEY   60 mL

VINAIGRETTE (3/4 CUP/175 mL OLIVE OIL
    TO 1/4 CUP/60 mL WINE VINEGAR)

FRESHLY GROUND PEPPER

ARRANGE SLICED TOMATOES AND CHEESE ALTERNATELY ON A PLATTER. SPRINKLE WITH BASIL, PARSLEY AND VINAIGRETTE. PASS THE PEPPER MILL!

THE ARGUMENT YOU WON FROM YOUR SPOUSE ISN'T OVER YET.

CRAB 'N' PASTA WITH GINGER DRESSING

THE LADIES DO LUNCH.

8 OZ. UNCOOKED PASTA, ROTINI OR FUSILLI	250 g
2 CUPS FRESH CRABMEAT	500 mL
½ CUP WATER CHESTNUTS, CHOPPED	125 mL
¼ CUP CHOPPED CELERY	60 mL
½ CUP SLICED CUCUMBER	125 mL
½ RED PEPPER, SLICED	
½ GREEN PEPPER, SLICED	

DRESSING

1 TBSP. GRATED FRESH GINGER	15 mL
⅓ CUP MAYONNAISE	75 mL
⅓ CUP SOUR CREAM OR PLAIN YOGURT	75 mL
½ TSP. FRESHLY GROUND PEPPER	2 mL
1 TBSP. SOY SAUCE	15 mL
1 TSP. SUGAR	5 mL
DASH RED PEPPER SAUCE	
LEAF LETTUCE	

COOK PASTA, DRAIN AND RINSE IN COLD WATER. COOL. COMBINE DRESSING INGREDIENTS AND BLEND. ADD REMAINING INGREDIENTS TO PASTA AND TOSS WITH DRESSING. ARRANGE ON LETTUCE LEAVES. FLAKY FREEZER BISCUITS (PAGE 28) ARE GREAT WITH THIS SALAD. SERVES 4-6.

A FOOL AND HIS MONEY ARE BETTER THAN NO DATE AT ALL.

TWO-TONE MELON SOUP

THE LUNCH BUNCH ARE GOING TO LOVE YOU FOR THIS ELEGANT BUT LOW-CAL. STARTER.

3½ CUPS CUBED CANTALOUPE (APPROXIMATELY 2)	825 mL
1 TBSP. LEMON JUICE	15 mL
3½ CUPS CUBED HONEYDEW MELON (APPROXIMATELY 1½)	825 mL
1 TBSP. LIME JUICE	15 mL
4 TSP. SUGAR	20 mL
6 TSP. PLAIN YOGURT	30 mL
MINT SPRIGS	

COMBINE CANTALOUPE, LEMON JUICE AND 2 TSP. SUGAR IN BLENDER. BLEND UNTIL SMOOTH AND THICK. TRANSFER TO A POURING VESSEL (THAT'LL BE YOUR PITCHER!). CHILL. COMBINE HONEYDEW, LIME JUICE AND 2 TSP. SUGAR. BLEND UNTIL SMOOTH AND THICK. TRANSFER TO A SECOND PITCHER AND CHILL.

TO SERVE: CHILL BOWLS. HOLDING A PITCHER IN EACH HAND (BETTER THAN A SECOND BASEMAN), POUR A GENEROUS ⅓ CUP OF EACH, SIDE BY SIDE INTO BOWL. GARNISH EACH BOWL WITH 1 TSP. OF YOGURT AND SWIRL IT IN AN "S" SHAPE WITH A KNIFE. SERVE WITH MINT. SERVES 6.

DEFINITION OF A GENTLEMAN: A MAN WHO CAN PLAY AN ACCORDION, BUT DOESN'T.

COLD STRAWBERRY SOUP

THIS IS EASY AND ELEGANT FOR A COOL PATIO LUNCH.

3 CUPS ROSÉ WINE	750 mL
4 CUPS SLICED STRAWBERRIES	1 L
½ CUP SUGAR	125 mL
2 CUPS SOUR CREAM OR LOW-FAT PLAIN YOGURT	500 mL
EXTRA SOUR CREAM OR YOGURT FOR GARNISH	

SIMMER WINE, STRAWBERRIES AND SUGAR FOR 30 MINUTES. CHILL. ADD SOUR CREAM OR YOGURT. PURÉE IN BLENDER OR FOOD PROCESSOR. STORE IN REFRIGERATOR UNTIL SERVING TIME.
SERVES 8.

ORTHODONTIA: THE DENTAL TECHNIQUE THAT KEEPS CHILDREN BRACED AND PARENTS STRAPPED.

CREAM OF TOMATO SOUP

HERE'S AN OLD-TIME FAVORITE - AND MIGHTY TASTY TOO!

2 - 19 OZ. CANS TOMATOES	2 - 540 mL
1 LARGE ONION, FINELY CHOPPED	
1 CUP CHOPPED CELERY	250 mL
10 OZ. CAN CHICKEN BROTH	284 mL
½ CUP SPICY CLAMATO JUICE	125 mL
1 TSP. DILL	5 mL
¼ CUP BUTTER OR MARGARINE	60 mL
½ CUP FLOUR	125 mL
4 CUPS MILK	1 L
1 CUP CHEESE WHIZ	250 mL
PARSLEY	

SIMMER TOMATOES, ONION, CELERY, BROTH, CLAMATO JUICE AND DILL UNTIL VEGGIES ARE COOKED, ABOUT 20 MINUTES. IN A MEDIUM-SIZED PAN, MELT BUTTER AND BLEND IN FLOUR TO MAKE A PASTE. ADD MILK SLOWLY, STIRRING CONSTANTLY, TO MAKE A THICK WHITE SAUCE. STIR IN VEGETABLE MIXTURE. FOLD IN CHEESE WHIZ AND GARNISH WITH PARSLEY. SERVES 4-6.

SHE HAS A GOOD HEAD ON HER SHOULDERS, ALTHOUGH IT WOULD LOOK BETTER ON HER NECK.

WELL WORTH THE EFFORT! THE PERFECT LIGHT LUNCHEON STARTER SERVED HOT OR COLD. MAY BE PREPARED THE DAY BEFORE.

4 LARGE RED PEPPERS	
2 TBSP. BUTTER OR MARGARINE	30 mL
1 LARGE RED ONION, CHOPPED	
2 GARLIC CLOVES, MINCED	
4 CUPS CHICKEN BROTH	1 L
1 TBSP. LEMON JUICE OR GIN	15 mL
SALT TO TASTE	
1/2 TSP. GROUND PEPPER	2 mL
SWEET BASIL	

CUT PEPPERS IN HALF AND REMOVE SEEDS. PLACE CUT SIDE DOWN ON A COOKIE SHEET. BROIL UNTIL SKINS ARE BLACKENED AND PUFFED. REMOVE FROM SHEET AND PLACE IN A PLASTIC BAG TO STEAM. SAUTÉ ONIONS AND GARLIC IN BUTTER UNTIL SOFT. REMOVE COOLED PEPPERS FROM BAG AND PEEL OFF SKINS. CUT INTO CHUNKS AND ADD TO ONIONS AND GARLIC. COOK FOR 2-3 MINUTES. ADD BROTH, COVER AND SIMMER 20 MINUTES. ADD LEMON JUICE OR GIN. IN A BLENDER OR FOOD PROCESSOR, WHIRL 1/3 OF THE MIXTURE AT A TIME UNTIL SMOOTH. (STRAIN IF YOU WISH.) SEASON WITH SALT AND PEPPER. GARNISH WITH BASIL. SERVES 4-6.

(SEE PICTURE - PAGE 53.)

BOY - A NOISE WITH DIRT ON IT.

CHEDDAR CORN CHOWDER

A COLD WINTER'S NIGHT, A FIRE AND THOU!

3 TBSP. BUTTER	45 mL
1 ONION, CHOPPED	
1 LARGE POTATO, PEELED & DICED	
1 BAY LEAF	
½ TSP. GROUND CUMIN	2 mL
¼ TSP. SAGE	1 mL
2 TBSP. FLOUR	30 mL
2 CUPS CHICKEN STOCK	500 mL
1¼ CUPS LIGHT CREAM	300 mL
1½ CUPS FROZEN CORN NIBLETS OR	375 mL
CANNED, DRAINED	
2 TBSP. CHOPPED FRESH PARSLEY	30 mL
2 TBSP. CHOPPED GREEN ONIONS	30 mL
¼ TSP. NUTMEG	1 mL
¼ CUP DRY WHITE WINE	60 mL
2 CUPS GRATED CHEDDAR CHEESE	500 mL
3-4 SLICES BACON, COOKED & CRUMBLED	

MELT BUTTER. ADD ONION, POTATO, BAY LEAF, CUMIN AND SAGE. COOK STIRRING FOR ABOUT 5 MINUTES. BLEND IN FLOUR AND THEN WHISK IN STOCK AND CREAM. BRING TO BOIL AND REDUCE HEAT AND SIMMER 30 MINUTES, STIRRING OFTEN. ADD CORN, PARSLEY, ONIONS, NUTMEG AND WINE. SIMMER FOR ANOTHER 5 MINUTES UNTIL HEATED THROUGH. REMOVE BAY LEAF. STIR IN CHEESE AND HEAT UNTIL MELTED (DO NOT BOIL). GARNISH WITH BACON BITS. SERVES 4.

ARTHRITIS: TWINGES IN THE HINGES.

CARROT SOUP

A GREAT BEGINNING FOR AN ELEGANT ENTRÉE!

1/4 CUP BUTTER	60 mL
2 CUPS FINELY CHOPPED ONION	500 mL
12 LARGE CARROTS, PEELED & SLICED	
4 CUPS CHICKEN STOCK	1 L
1 CUP FRESH ORANGE JUICE	250 mL
SALT & PEPPER TO TASTE	
ORANGE ZEST	

MELT BUTTER IN POT AND ADD ONIONS, COOKING OVER LOW HEAT UNTIL LIGHTLY BROWNED. ADD CARROTS AND STOCK AND BRING TO A BOIL. REDUCE HEAT. COVER AND COOK UNTIL CARROTS ARE VERY TENDER, ABOUT 30 MINUTES. POUR THROUGH A STRAINER, RESERVING STOCK. ADD STRAINED VEGETABLES IN BATCHES TO FOOD PROCESSOR OR BLENDER AND PURÉE UNTIL SMOOTH. RETURN PURÉE TO POT, ADD ORANGE JUICE AND RESERVED STOCK. SEASON TO TASTE. ADD ORANGE ZEST. SIMMER UNTIL HEATED THROUGH. SERVES 6-8.

GOSSIP: A PERSON WHO TELLS THINGS BEFORE YOU HAVE A CHANCE TO TELL THEM.

PUMPKIN SOUP

Sometimes known as mystery soup! What is this orange stuff anyway?

1 small onion, chopped	
2 cups sliced mushrooms	500 mL
¼ cup butter	60 mL
¼ cup flour	60 mL
4 cups chicken broth	1 L
1 cup canned pumpkin (not pie filling)	250 mL
1 cup light cream	250 mL
2 tbsp. honey	30 mL
1 tsp. nutmeg	5 mL
croûtons	

In a large pot, sauté onion and mushrooms in butter for 1-2 minutes. Remove from heat. Stir in flour. Add chicken broth and pumpkin and bring to a boil. Reduce heat and simmer for 20 minutes. Stir in cream, honey and nutmeg. Serve with croûtons sprinkled on top. Serves 4.

BOUILLABAISSE - A FINE KETTLE OF FISH.

TUSCAN MINESTRONE

WHILST CYCLING IN TUSCANY . . .

1 MEDIUM ONION, CHOPPED	
4 GARLIC CLOVES, MINCED	
2 TBSP. OLIVE OIL	30 mL
½ LB. LEAN GROUND VEAL (BEEF WILL DO)	250 g
3 ROMA TOMATOES, CHOPPED	
2 STALKS CELERY, CHOPPED	
3 CARROTS, THINLY SLICED	
1 MEDIUM ZUCCHINI, CHOPPED	
28 OZ. CAN ROMA TOMATOES, BLENDED BRIEFLY AT LOW SPEED	796 mL
28 OZ. CAN WATER	796 mL
1 TBSP. OREGANO	15 mL
SALT & PEPPER TO TASTE	
19 OZ. CAN WHITE KIDNEY BEANS	540 mL
1 MEDIUM POTATO, PEELED & CHOPPED	
1 CUP FRESHLY GRATED PARMESAN CHEESE	250 mL
½ CUP CHOPPED FRESH PARSLEY	125 mL

SAUTÉ ONION AND GARLIC IN OLIVE OIL. ADD VEAL AND COOK FOR 5 MINUTES. ADD TOMATOES, CELERY, CARROTS AND ZUCCHINI. COOK, STIRRING OCCASIONALLY, FOR 20 MINUTES. ADD CANNED TOMATOES, WATER AND SEASONINGS. SIMMER, UNCOVERED, ON LOW FOR 30 MINUTES. ADD KIDNEY BEANS AND POTATO AND SIMMER, UNCOVERED, ANOTHER 10-15 MINUTES OR UNTIL POTATO IS FORK-TENDER. SERVE WITH A SPRINKLE OF PARMESAN AND PARSLEY. SERVES 8-10 TUSCANS - AND WE LIKE IT TOO!

BEST OF BRIDGE BEAN SOUP

Your next family favorite! The very thing for a cold winter's night.

1 lb. hot Italian sausage	500 g
2 smoked pork hocks or 2-3 cups cubed ham	
3 medium potatoes, peeled & cubed	
2 medium onions, diced	
3 celery stalks with leaves, chopped	
5 carrots, peeled & diced	
1 green pepper, seeded & chopped	
1 cup chopped parsley or 2 tbsp. (30 mL) dried	250 mL
3 - 14 oz. cans kidney beans	3 - 398 mL
14 oz. can tomato sauce	398 mL
28 oz. can tomatoes, chopped	796 mL
1-2 tsp. salt	5-10 mL
1 tsp. pepper	5 mL
1 tsp. hot pepper sauce	5 mL
2 bay leaves	
1 tsp. Worcestershire sauce	5 mL
2 garlic cloves, crushed	

Boil sausage to remove excess fat and cut into bite-sized pieces. Skin pork hocks and remove excess fat. Brown sausage and pork hocks in a large, heavy pot. Drain. Add all other ingredients and add just enough water to cover. Bring to a boil then reduce to simmer. Cover and continue to cook for 2-3 hours. Remove pork hocks and cut meat into bite-sized pieces. Return meat to pot. Serve with crusty bread or cheddar beer bread (page 25). Serves 8-10. (See cover picture.)

"RATATOOEE!"

A vegetarian tootee.

2 TBSP. OLIVE OIL	30 mL
1 TBSP. BUTTER	15 mL
4 LARGE ONIONS, THINLY SLICED	
12 MEDIUM MUSHROOMS, SLICED	
3 SMALL EGGPLANTS (FIRM & SHINY), PEELED & SLICED 1/4" THICK	
OLIVE OIL	
SALT & PEPPER TO TASTE	
4 LARGE TOMATOES, PEELED & SLICED	
BASIL	
PARMESAN CHEESE	
HERBED BREAD CRUMBS	
1 CUP GRATED MOZZARELLA CHEESE	250 mL

HEAT OIL AND BUTTER IN A HEAVY FRYING PAN; ADD ONIONS AND SAUTÉ OVER MEDIUM HEAT UNTIL SOFT. REMOVE AND SET ASIDE. IN THE SAME PAN SAUTÉ MUSHROOMS. ARRANGE EGGPLANT SLICES CLOSE TOGETHER ON A COOKIE SHEET AND BRUSH WITH OLIVE OIL. BROIL IN OVEN (BOTH SIDES) UNTIL SLICES APPEAR LIGHTLY TOASTED. USING A LARGE CASSEROLE, LAYER 1/3 OF THE EGGPLANT SLICES SEASONED WITH SALT AND PEPPER. LAYER WITH 1/2 THE ONIONS, THEN 1/2 OF THE MUSHROOMS AND A FEW SLICES OF TOMATO. SEASON TOMATOES WITH SALT AND PEPPER AND A SPRINKLING OF BASIL AND PARMESAN CHEESE. REPEAT LAYERS

"RATATOOEE!"

THIS RECIPE CONTINUED FROM PAGE 74.

UNTIL ALL INGREDIENTS HAVE BEEN USED, ENDING WITH EGGPLANT. SPRINKLE BREAD CRUMBS OVER THE TOP. COVER WITH MOZZARELLA CHEESE. BAKE FOR ONE HOUR AT 350°F. SERVES 6-8.

CELERY SAUTÉ

A GOOD COMPANY VEGGIE - QUICK AND EASY.

3 TBSP. BUTTER OR MARGARINE	45 mL
3-4 MEDIUM STALKS OF CELERY, CUT IN THIN 3" STRIPS	
4 GREEN ONIONS, CHOPPED	
1-4 GARLIC CLOVES, MINCED	
½ CUP TOASTED SLIVERED ALMONDS	125 mL

USING A HEAVY SKILLET, MELT BUTTER AND ADD THE CELERY. SAUTÉ FOR 3 MINUTES, STIRRING CONSTANTLY. ADD THE GREEN ONIONS AND GARLIC. SAUTÉ A BIT LONGER, STILL STIRRING CONSTANTLY, BUT DO NOT OVERCOOK; THE CELERY SHOULD BE SOMEWHAT CRISP. COMBINE WITH TOASTED ALMONDS AND SPRINKLE A FEW ON TOP. SERVES 4.

BARBER'S BEST CHILI

A VEGETARIAN VERSION.

1½ CUPS CHOPPED ONION	375 mL
2 GREEN PEPPERS, SEEDED & CHOPPED	
3 CELERY STALKS, CHOPPED	
4 GARLIC CLOVES, MINCED	
2 TBSP. OIL	30mL
2 - 28 OZ. CANS TOMATOES	2 - 796 mL
14 OZ. CAN KIDNEY BEANS	398 mL
14 OZ. CAN BROWN BEANS	398 mL
2 CUPS SLICED FRESH MUSHROOMS	500 mL
1½ CUPS WATER	375 mL
½ CUP RAISINS	125 mL
¼ CUP VINEGAR	60 mL
1 BAY LEAF	
1 TBSP. CHILI POWDER	15 mL
1 TBSP. PARSLEY	15 mL
1½ TSP. BASIL	7 mL
1½ TSP. OREGANO	7 mL
½ TSP. PEPPER	2 mL
¼ TSP. TABASCO	1 mL
1 CUP CASHEWS (OPTIONAL)	250 mL
GRATED CHEDDAR CHEESE	
SOUR CREAM	

SAUTÉ ONION, GREEN PEPPER, CELERY, GARLIC IN OIL UNTIL TENDER. ADD TOMATOES AND BEANS WITH LIQUID, ALONG WITH REMAINING INGREDIENTS, EXCEPT CASHEWS, CHEESE AND SOUR CREAM. COVER AND SIMMER FOR ONE HOUR. UNCOVER AND SIMMER ANOTHER HOUR. REMOVE BAY LEAF (IF YOU CAN FIND IT). IF USING CASHEWS, ADD AT THE END. SERVE WITH GRATED CHEDDAR CHEESE AND A DOLLOP OF SOUR CREAM. SERVES 8-10 - DEPENDING ON WHAT SIZE YOUR BARBERS ARE!

GARLIC HERBED POTATOES

SMOOTH AND CREAMY!

7-10 POTATOES, PEELED & QUARTERED	
8 GARLIC CLOVES, PEELED	
PINCH OF SALT	
3/4 CUP SOUR CREAM, ROOM TEMPERATURE	175 mL
2 TBSP. BUTTER	30 mL
1/3 CUP CHOPPED FRESH PARSLEY	75 mL
PEPPER TO TASTE	

PLACE POTATOES IN A LARGE POT OF WATER WITH GARLIC AND SALT. COOK, COVERED, 20-30 MINUTES OR UNTIL TENDER. DRAIN WELL. RETURN POTATOES TO POT OVER HEAT FOR AT LEAST ONE MINUTE TO DRY OUT EXCESS MOISTURE. MASH POTATOES, ADD SOUR CREAM AND BUTTER, BEATING UNTIL SMOOTH. STIR IN PARSLEY AND PEPPER. SERVES 8.

ROASTED NEW POTATOES WITH HERBS

HERB AND ROSEMARY MAKE A NICE COUPLE!

8 MEDIUM NEW POTATOES	
1/4 CUP OLIVE OIL	60 mL
2-3 GARLIC CLOVES, CRUSHED	
2 TBSP. DRIED HERBS (ROSEMARY OR MINT)	30 mL

WASH POTATOES AND CUT INTO QUARTERS. ARRANGE IN SHALLOW BAKING DISH AND TOSS WITH OIL, GARLIC AND HERBS. BAKE AT 375°F FOR ONE HOUR, TURNING OCCASIONALLY. SERVES 4-6.

SWISS POTATOES

SOUND YOUR ALP HORN!

8 MEDIUM RED POTATOES, THINLY SLICED, CHILLED IN COLD WATER	
SALT & PEPPER TO TASTE	
2-3 CUPS GRATED SWISS CHEESE	500-750 mL
6 TBSP. BUTTER	90 mL
1 CUP CHICKEN STOCK	250 mL

PREHEAT OVEN TO 425°F. GREASE A 9" X 13" DISH. PAT POTATOES DRY AND ARRANGE HALF OF THE POTATOES IN DISH. SPRINKLE WITH SALT, PEPPER AND HALF THE CHEESE AND DOT WITH HALF THE BUTTER. REPEAT LAYER. POUR STOCK OVER TOP. BAKE 45-60 MINUTES OR UNTIL POTATOES ARE TENDER AND TOP IS GOLDEN. SERVES 6.

CRISPY OVEN-BAKED POTATOES

3 CUPS CORNFLAKES	750 mL
3 TBSP. GRATED PARMESAN CHEESE	45 mL
1 TSP. PAPRIKA	5 mL
¼ TSP. GARLIC SALT	1 mL
2 LARGE BAKING POTATOES, PEELED & SLICED	
¼ CUP BUTTER OR MARGARINE, MELTED	60 mL

PREHEAT OVEN TO 375°F. PROCESS CORNFLAKES, CHEESE AND SPICES IN BLENDER. DIP POTATOES IN BUTTER AND THEN IN CORNFLAKE MIXTURE. PLACE ON A WELL-GREASED BAKING SHEET. BAKE 20-25 MINUTES. SERVES 4.

DRESSED UP SPUDS

5 MEDIUM POTATOES
½ LB. BACON, CUT IN PIECES   250 g
1 LARGE ONION, SLICED
8 OZ. BOTTLE CREAMY ITALIAN DRESSING   250 mL
     OR CREAMY CUCUMBER DRESSING
½ CUP GRATED SWISS CHEESE   125 mL

PEEL POTATOES AND CHOP IN CHUNKS. BOIL 20 MINUTES. COOL. FRY BACON UNTIL CRISP AND ONION UNTIL SOFT. GREASE A 4-CUP CASSEROLE. LAYER POTATOES WITH BACON AND ONION MIXTURE. POUR DRESSING OVER ALL. SPRINKLE WITH CHEESE AND BAKE IN A PREHEATED 325°F OVEN FOR AN HOUR OR UNTIL BUBBLY. SERVES 6.

OVEN-BAKED FRIES

A HEALTHIER WAY TO ENJOY THE ALL-TIME FAVORITE FRENCH FRY!

4 MEDIUM POTATOES, UNPEELED
1-2 TBSP. VEGETABLE OIL   15-30 mL
LAWRY'S SEASONED SALT

PREHEAT OVEN TO 475°F. WASH POTATOES, SLICE INTO ½" STRIPS, PAT DRY. TOSS POTATOES WITH OIL IN A BOWL TO COAT. SPREAD ON BAKING SHEET AND SPRINKLE WITH SEASONED SALT. BAKE FOR 30 MINUTES. TURN OCCASIONALLY.

LEMON RICE

SEVEN OUT OF TEN CHICKENS WOULD RATHER BE SEEN WITH LEMON RICE.

2½ CUPS CHICKEN BROTH	625 mL
1 CUP UNCOOKED RICE	250 mL
1 GARLIC CLOVE, CRUSHED	
1 TBSP. CHOPPED FRESH LEMON RIND	15 mL
2 TBSP. DILL	30 mL
2 TBSP. BUTTER	30 mL

MIX BROTH, RICE AND GARLIC IN SAUCEPAN. BRING TO BOIL, COVER AND REDUCE HEAT. COOK ON LOW HEAT FOR 20-30 MINUTES UNTIL LIQUID IS ABSORBED. ADD LEMON RIND, DILL AND BUTTER. SERVE WITH CHICKEN OR FISH. SERVES 6. (SEE PICTURE - PAGE 121.)

TEENAGER: FOOLING MY MOM IS LIKE TRYING TO SNEAK A SUNRISE PAST A ROOSTER.

ORZO WITH PARMESAN & BASIL

THE PASTA THAT LOOKS LIKE RICE - GREAT WITH CHICKEN OR FISH.

3 TBSP. BUTTER	45 mL
1½ CUPS ORZO	375 mL
3 CUPS CHICKEN BROTH	750 mL
½ CUP GRATED PARMESAN CHEESE	125 mL
6 TBSP. CHOPPED FRESH BASIL OR	90 mL
1½ TSP. (7 mL) DRIED	
SALT & PEPPER TO TASTE	

MELT BUTTER IN SKILLET OVER MEDIUM-HIGH HEAT. ADD ORZO AND SAUTÉ 2 MINUTES UNTIL SLIGHTLY BROWN. ADD STOCK AND BRING TO A BOIL. REDUCE HEAT, COVER AND SIMMER UNTIL ORZO IS TENDER AND LIQUID IS ABSORBED, ABOUT 20 MINUTES. MIX IN PARMESAN AND BASIL. SEASON WITH SALT AND PEPPER. TRANSFER TO SHALLOW BOWL. SERVES 6. (SEE PICTURE - PAGE 103.)

VARIATION: FOR A CREAMIER PASTA DISH, TRY STIRRING IN 2 TBSP. PLAIN YOGURT THINNED WITH A LITTLE MILK.

BEFORE T.V. NOBODY KNEW WHAT A HEADACHE LOOKED LIKE.

RISOTTO

THE CLASSIC COMPLEMENT TO OSSO BUCO (PAGE 108).

½ CUP BUTTER OR MARGARINE	125	mL
½ CUP FINELY CHOPPED ONION	125	mL
1½ CUPS UNCOOKED RICE	375	mL
3½ CUPS CHICKEN BROTH	825	mL
½ CUP DRY WHITE WINE	125	mL
1 TSP. CRUSHED SAFFRON	5	mL
2 TBSP. CHICKEN BROTH	30	mL
2 TBSP. FRESHLY GRATED PARMESAN CHEESE	30	mL

MELT ¼ CUP BUTTER IN MEDIUM SAUCEPAN AND SAUTÉ ONION UNTIL TRANSPARENT. ADD THE RICE AND STIR TO MIX. ADD BROTH AND WINE AND BRING TO BOIL. COVER AND COOK OVER LOW HEAT FOR 25 MINUTES, STIRRING OCCASIONALLY. STIR IN ¼ CUP OF BUTTER. SOFTEN SAFFRON IN 2 TBSP. OF CHICKEN BROTH, ADD TO RICE AND COOK, UNCOVERED, OVER LOW HEAT FOR 5 MORE MINUTES. TO SERVE, SPRINKLE WITH PARMESAN CHEESE. SERVES 6-8.

IF WE HAD AS LITTLE ON OUR MINDS AS ELEPHANTS DO, WE COULD REMEMBER TOO.

CARROTS WITH ARTICHOKE HEARTS

2 CUPS QUARTERED FRESH MUSHROOMS	500 mL
1 TBSP. OLIVE OIL	15 mL
1½ TBSP. BUTTER	22 mL
SALT & FRESHLY GROUND PEPPER	
2 TBSP. MINCED SHALLOTS OR GREEN ONIONS	30 mL
9 OZ. PKG. FROZEN ARTICHOKE HEARTS, COOKED	255 g
1 LB. SLICED CARROTS OR 3 CUPS (750 mL) BABY CARROTS, COOKED TENDER CRISP	500 g
⅓ CUP BEEF STOCK	75 mL
2 TBSP. MINCED PARSLEY OR A COMBINATION OF PARSLEY, CHERVIL & CHIVES	30 mL

SAUTÉ THE MUSHROOMS IN THE OIL AND BUTTER IN A SKILLET, UNTIL VERY LIGHTLY BROWNED. SEASON WITH SALT AND PEPPER. STIR SHALLOTS AND ARTICHOKE HEARTS INTO THE MUSHROOMS AND COOK FOR 2 OR 3 MINUTES OVER MEDIUM-HIGH HEAT. GENTLY STIR IN THE CARROTS. ADD THE STOCK TO THE MIXTURE AND COVER. COOK SLOWLY FOR 4 OR 5 MINUTES, UNTIL THE STOCK HAS ALMOST EVAPORATED. CORRECT SEASONINGS. PUT THE VEGETABLES IN A HOT SERVING DISH AND SPRINKLE WITH PARSLEY. SERVES 6.

MY GOLF IS IMPROVING. YESTERDAY I HIT THE BALL IN ONE.

CARROT PATCH

ELMER FUDD'S FINEST

5 CUPS SLICED, PEELED CARROTS	1.25 L
2 TSP. LEMON JUICE	10 mL
2 TBSP. MINCED ONION	30 mL
½ CUP BUTTER, SOFTENED	125 mL
¼ CUP SUGAR	60 mL
1 TBSP. FLOUR	15 mL
1 TSP. SALT	5 mL
¼ TSP. CINNAMON	1 mL
1 CUP MILK	250 mL
3 EGGS	

COOK AND PURÉE CARROTS. ADD LEMON JUICE AND COVER TIGHTLY UNTIL READY TO MIX. BEAT REMAINING INGREDIENTS UNTIL SMOOTH. STIR IN CARROT PURÉE. POUR INTO GREASED 2-QUART SOUFFLÉ DISH. BAKE, UNCOVERED, AT 350°F, 45 MINUTES TO ONE HOUR, UNTIL CENTER IS FIRM. GREAT SERVED WITH TURKEY, HAM OR PORK ROAST. SERVES 6.

DON'T MAKE THE GARDEN TOO BIG IF YOUR WIFE TIRES EASILY.

PERFECT PEPPERS

A COLORFUL COMPANION FOR FISH OR CHICKEN.

2 CUPS SMALL SHELL PASTA	500 mL
4 LARGE PEPPERS - RED, YELLOW & GREEN	
1 TBSP. OIL	15 mL
½ CUP CHOPPED FRESH BASIL	125 mL
3-4 GARLIC CLOVES, MINCED	
1 TBSP. CAPERS	15 mL
4 ANCHOVIES, CHOPPED	
2 TBSP. CHOPPED CHIVES OR GREEN ONIONS	30 mL
4 ROMA TOMATOES, CHOPPED	
2 SHALLOTS, FINELY CHOPPED	
2 CUPS GRATED MOZZARELLA CHEESE	500 mL
SALT & PEPPER TO TASTE	

COOK PASTA ACCORDING TO PACKAGE DIRECTIONS. DRAIN AND SET ASIDE. HALVE PEPPERS LENGTHWISE. REMOVE SEEDS AND SET IN A GREASED SHALLOW CASSEROLE. MIX PASTA WITH REMAINING INGREDIENTS AND PILE INTO PEPPER HALVES. BAKE AT 350°F FOR 40 MINUTES.

HOW CAN THERE BE SO MUCH DIFFERENCE BETWEEN A DAY OFF AND AN OFF DAY?

SPICY SPAGHETTI SQUASH

1 MEDIUM SPAGHETTI SQUASH	
½ CUP BUTTER OR MARGARINE, SOFTENED	125 mL
3 TBSP. PACKED BROWN SUGAR	45 mL
¼ TSP. EACH: CINNAMON, ALLSPICE &	1 mL
NUTMEG	

CUT SQUASH IN HALF LENGTHWISE; SCOOP OUT AND DISCARD SEEDS. PLACE CUT SIDE DOWN IN BAKING DISH, ADD ¼ CUP OF WATER. MICROWAVE ON HIGH FOR AT LEAST 15 MINUTES OR BAKE AT 350° F FOR 30 MINUTES OR UNTIL SKIN IS SOFT. IN A SMALL BOWL MIX REMAINING INGREDIENTS. WHEN SQUASH IS COOKED, PULL STRANDS FREE WITH A FORK, PLACE IN SERVING BOWL AND MIX WITH SPICY BUTTER. GREAT WITH HAM! SERVES 5.

AN ALTERNATE WAY TO SERVE: SPRINKLE SQUASH WITH SALT, PEPPER AND FRESHLY GRATED PARMESAN.

IF WOMEN ARE SO SMART, WHY DO THEY ALWAYS DANCE BACKWARDS?

MUSHROOMS AU GRATIN

SERVE AS A SIDE DISH WITH ROAST BEEF OR
ON A BURGER.

2 TBSP. BUTTER	30 mL
1 LB. MUSHROOMS, SLICED	500 g
1/3 CUP SOUR CREAM	75 mL
1/4 TSP. SALT	1 mL
DASH OF PEPPER	
1 TBSP. FLOUR	15 mL
1/4 CUP FINELY CHOPPED PARSLEY	60 mL
1/2 CUP GRATED SWISS OR MOZZARELLA	125 mL
CHEESE OR HALF OF EACH	

MELT BUTTER OVER MEDIUM-HIGH HEAT AND
SAUTÉ MUSHROOMS. BLEND SOUR CREAM, SALT,
PEPPER AND FLOUR. STIR INTO MUSHROOMS.
HEAT UNTIL IT BEGINS TO BOIL. REMOVE FROM
HEAT AND POUR INTO A SHALLOW BAKING DISH.
SPRINKLE PARSLEY AND CHEESE ON TOP. BAKE
AT 425°F UNTIL HEATED THROUGH, ABOUT 10
MINUTES.

BAD HOUSEKEEPING - THE MAGAZINE FOR
WOMEN WHO COULD CARE LESS.

SAUCY BRUSSELS SPROUTS

CHEEKY LITTLE DEVILS!

2-3 CUPS BRUSSELS SPROUTS	500-750 mL
¼ CUP BUTTER	60 mL
¼ CUP FINELY CHOPPED ONION	60 mL
PINCH OF SUGAR	
1 TBSP. RED WINE OR BURGUNDY COOKING WINE	15 mL
2 TBSP. CHOPPED FRESH PARSLEY	30 mL
2 TBSP. DIJON MUSTARD	30 mL
SALT & PEPPER TO TASTE	

SIMMER SPROUTS, UNCOVERED, ABOUT 10 MINUTES. WHILE SPROUTS ARE COOKING, PREPARE SAUCE BY MELTING BUTTER AND SAUTÉ ONIONS UNTIL SOFT. ADD REMAINING INGREDIENTS AND STIR TO BLEND. POUR OVER COOKED SPROUTS AND PLACE IN SERVING DISH. YUM! SERVES 4.

MY WIFE RAN OFF WITH MY BEST FRIEND, AND I STILL MISS HIM A LOT.

GREEN BEANS VINAIGRETTE

CRUNCHY COLD VEGGIE FOR A HOT SUMMER'S DAY.

3 LBS. FRESH GREEN BEANS	1.5 kg
1 TBSP. GRATED ONION	15 mL
½ TSP. SALT	2 mL
¾ TSP. FRESHLY GROUND PEPPER	4 mL
1 TBSP. DIJON MUSTARD	15 mL
3 TBSP. WHITE WINE VINEGAR	45 mL
½ CUP OLIVE OIL	125 mL
½ TSP. LEMON JUICE	2 mL

COOK BEANS JUST UNTIL TENDER CRISP. RINSE IN COLD WATER AND CHILL. COMBINE REMAINING INGREDIENTS, EXCEPT OLIVE OIL AND LEMON JUICE. GRADUALLY WHISK IN OIL AND LEMON JUICE. POUR OVER BEANS AND MARINATE IN FRIDGE AT LEAST 4 HOURS. SERVES 12.

GREAT WITH WILD WEST SALMON (PAGE 125).

I NEVER RAN AWAY AS A CHILD - OF COURSE, I NEVER DID ANYTHING ELSE MY PARENTS WANTED ME TO DO.

GREEN BEANS GUIDO

¼ CUP VEGETABLE OIL	60 mL
4 CUPS SLICED FRESH MUSHROOMS	1 L
2 TBSP. CHOPPED ONIONS	30 mL
1 GARLIC CLOVE, MINCED	
1 RED PEPPER, SEEDED & CHOPPED	
10 OZ. PKG. FROZEN WHOLE GREEN BEANS	283 g
1 TBSP. CHOPPED FRESH BASIL	15 mL
OR 1½ TSP. (7 mL) DRY	
½ CUP GRATED PARMESAN CHEESE	125 mL

HEAT OIL IN LARGE SKILLET OVER MEDIUM HEAT. ADD MUSHROOMS, ONION, GARLIC AND RED PEPPER. COOK UNTIL ONION IS LIMP, ABOUT 5 MINUTES. ADD BEANS AND BASIL. CONTINUE TO COOK, STIRRING FREQUENTLY, UNTIL BEANS ARE TENDER CRISP, ABOUT 10 MINUTES. ADD SEVERAL SPOONFULS OF CHEESE AND MIX WELL. PLACE IN SHALLOW CASSEROLE AND SPRINKLE REMAINING CHEESE ON TOP. SERVES 4.

A NEW MEDICAL THEORY IS THAT EXERCISE KILLS GERMS. THE TOUGH THING IS GETTING THE GERMS TO EXERCISE!

FRIED GREEN TOMATOES

SOUTHERN FIXINGS - IZZIE SAYS, "Y' ALL COME."

¼ CUP CORNMEAL	60 mL
1 TSP. SALT	5 mL
¼ TSP. PEPPER	1 mL
1 TSP. SUGAR	5 mL
1 EGG, BEATEN	
2 TBSP. WATER	30 mL
4 GREEN TOMATOES, SLICED ½" THICK	
¼ CUP BUTTER	60 mL

COMBINE CORNMEAL, SALT, PEPPER AND SUGAR. MIX EGG AND WATER. DIP TOMATOES INTO EGG MIXTURE THEN BOTH SIDES INTO CORNMEAL MIXTURE. HEAT BUTTER IN PAN AND FRY TOMATOES UNTIL GOLDEN. ADD MORE BUTTER AS NEEDED.

WHEN BUYING A COLD REMEDY, ALWAYS BUY THE CHEAPEST - THE EXPENSIVE ONES DON'T WORK EITHER!

NEVER-FAIL BLENDER HOLLANDAISE

1 CUP BUTTER	250 mL
4 EGG YOLKS	
¼ TSP. EACH: SALT, SUGAR, TABASCO & DRY MUSTARD	1 mL
2 TBSP. FRESH LEMON JUICE	30 mL

HEAT BUTTER TO A FULL BOIL, BEING CAREFUL NOT TO BROWN. COMBINE ALL OTHER INGREDIENTS IN BLENDER. WITH BLENDER TURNED ON HIGH, SLOWLY POUR BUTTER INTO YOLK MIXTURE IN A THIN STREAM UNTIL ALL IS ADDED. KEEPS WELL IN REFRIGERATOR FOR SEVERAL DAYS. WHEN REHEATING, HEAT OVER HOT (NOT BOILING) WATER IN TOP OF DOUBLE BOILER. MAKES ABOUT 1¼ CUPS OF SAUCE.

CREOLE SEASONING

SPICY HOT SEASONING FOR FISH, MEAT OR SEAFOOD.

2 TBSP. DRIED OREGANO	30 mL
⅓ CUP SALT	75 mL
¼ CUP GARLIC POWDER	60 mL
2-4 TBSP. BLACK PEPPER	30-60 mL
1-2 TBSP. CAYENNE PEPPER	15-30 mL
2 TBSP. DRIED THYME	30 mL
⅓ CUP PAPRIKA	75 mL
3 TBSP. ONION POWDER	45 mL

MIX ALL INGREDIENTS TOGETHER AND STORE IN AN AIRTIGHT CONTAINER. BEFORE COOKING, SPRINKLE OVER MEAT OF YOUR CHOICE. MAKES 1½ CUPS.

HOT AND SWEET MUSTARD

A MARVELOUS GIFT FOR YOUR CHRISTMAS EXCHANGE.

1 CUP DRY MUSTARD	250 mL
3/4 CUP SUGAR	175 mL
1 TSP. SALT	5 mL
1/4 TSP. WHITE PEPPER	1 mL
1/4 TSP. PAPRIKA	1 mL
1 CUP DRY WHITE WINE	250 mL
3 TBSP. WHITE VINEGAR	45 mL
2 EGG YOLKS	

MIX MUSTARD, SUGAR, SALT, PEPPER AND PAPRIKA IN A HEAVY PAN. GRADUALLY ADD WINE AND VINEGAR, COMBINING WELL. COOK, STIRRING CONSTANTLY, UNTIL BUBBLES START TO FORM ON TOP. BEAT EGG YOLKS IN A SEPARATE BOWL AND SLOWLY ADD ABOUT 1/2 CUP OF THE HOT MIXTURE TO YOLKS. RETURN EGG MIXTURE TO HOT MUSTARD AND WHISK WELL OVER MEDIUM HEAT UNTIL MIXTURE THICKENS. POUR INTO STERILIZED JARS. KEEPS UP TO 2 MONTHS IN REFRIGERATOR. MAKES 2 CUPS.

THIS CAN ALSO BE MADE IN THE MICROWAVE.

MARRIAGES ARE MADE IN HEAVEN - SO ARE THUNDER AND LIGHTNING.

CARROT MARMALADE

ANOTHER TASTY CHRISTMAS OR HOSTESS GIFT!
PUT INTO PRETTY JARS AND TIE WITH A RIBBON.

15 CUPS PEELED & CHOPPED CARROTS, ABOUT 4 LBS. (2 kg)	3.75 L
7 LEMONS, CHOPPED, PEEL & ALL	
7 ORANGES, CHOPPED, PEEL & ALL	
28 OZ. CAN CRUSHED PINEAPPLE	796 mL
12 CUPS SUGAR	3 L

FINELY GRIND CARROTS AND FRUITS IN A FOOD
PROCESSOR OR GRINDER. PUT IN A LARGE POT,
COVER WITH SUGAR AND LET STAND OVERNIGHT.
BOIL BRISKLY FOR 15 MINUTES. POUR INTO
STERILIZED JARS AND SEAL. MAKES LOTS.

COUNTRY MILE: THE DISTANCE BETWEEN AN
EMPTY GAS TANK AND THE NEAREST FILLING
STATION.

B.L.!'S BEST MUSTARD PICKLES

2 BUNCHES CELERY	
3 LARGE CUCUMBERS	
6 LARGE ONIONS	
1 LARGE CAULIFLOWER	
12 MEDIUM GREEN TOMATOES	
2 RED PEPPERS	
½ CUP PICKLING SALT	125 mL

DRESSING

8 CUPS WHITE SUGAR	2 L
⅔ CUP DRY MUSTARD	150 mL
1 TBSP. TURMERIC	15 mL
2 TBSP. CELERY SALT	30 mL
2 TBSP. CURRY POWDER	30 mL
1 CUP FLOUR	250 mL
2 CUPS MALT VINEGAR	500 mL
4 CUPS WHITE VINEGAR	1 L

CHOP ALL VEGETABLES AND MIX IN A LARGE POT OR ROASTER. COVER WITH PICKLING SALT AND LET STAND ONE HOUR. DRAIN OFF 2 CUPS OF LIQUID. MIX DRY INGREDIENTS TOGETHER IN A SAUCEPAN. ADD VINEGARS AND BOIL GENTLY UNTIL THICKENED. POUR OVER VEGETABLES. COOK FOR 10 MINUTES. COOL ANOTHER 10 MINUTES. POUR INTO STERILIZED JARS. MAKES APPROXIMATELY 10-12 PINTS.

PEOPLE ALWAYS SEEM TO DRIVE BETTER WHEN I'M NOT IN A RUSH.

CRANBERRY AND RAISIN CHUTNEY

2 CUPS WATER	500 mL
1 CUP RAISINS	250 mL
2 CUPS SUGAR	500 mL
2 TBSP. WHITE WINE VINEGAR	30 mL
1 CUP ORANGE JUICE	250 mL
2 TBSP. GRATED ORANGE ZEST	30 mL
2 TBSP. SLIVERED FRESH GINGER	30 mL
6 CUPS CRANBERRIES, FRESH OR FROZEN	1.5 L
2 PEARS, PEELED, CORED, CHOPPED	
1 CUP TOASTED SLIVERED ALMONDS	250 mL

BOIL WATER AND ADD RAISINS. REMOVE FROM HEAT AND LET STAND 20 MINUTES. DRAIN, RESERVING ½ CUP LIQUID. ADD SUGAR AND VINEGAR TO RAISIN WATER. HEAT IN SAUCEPAN UNTIL SUGAR DISSOLVES. INCREASE HEAT AND BOIL WITHOUT STIRRING UNTIL SYRUP TURNS GOLDEN BROWN, ABOUT 15 MINUTES. ADD ORANGE JUICE, ZEST, GINGER AND CRANBERRIES AND COOK ABOUT 10 MINUTES. STIR IN RAISINS, PEARS AND ALMONDS. POUR INTO STERILIZED JARS AND KEEP REFRIGERATED. MAKES ABOUT 6 CUPS.

WHENEVER I MEET A MAN WHO WOULD MAKE A GOOD HUSBAND - HE IS.

GREEN TOMATO MINCEMEAT

ALL YOU NEED IS A LARGE POT AND A DAY AT HOME. THE AROMA IS WONDERFUL AND YOUR TARTS WILL BE TOO.

6 CUPS FINELY CHOPPED GREEN TOMATOES	1.5 L
6 CUPS PEELED, FINELY CHOPPED TART APPLES	1.5 L
1 CUP GROUND SUET	250 mL
4 CUPS BROWN SUGAR	1 L
3 CUPS CURRANTS	750 mL
3 CUPS RAISINS	750 mL
1 CUP CHOPPED MIXED PEEL	250 mL
¾ CUP VINEGAR	175 mL
¼ CUP LEMON JUICE	60 mL
1 TSP. GROUND CLOVES	5 mL
1 TSP. ALLSPICE	5 mL
1 TBSP. CINNAMON	15 mL
2 TSP. SALT	10 mL
RUM TO TASTE (OPTIONAL)	

COVER TOMATOES WITH COLD WATER. BRING TO A BOIL AND DRAIN. REPEAT TWICE MORE, DISCARDING THE WATER EACH TIME. DRAIN WELL. ADD REMAINING INGREDIENTS EXCEPT RUM. BRING TO BOIL, REDUCE HEAT AND SIMMER, UNCOVERED, UNTIL MIXTURE THICKENS, AT LEAST 2 HOURS. ADD RUM. STORE IN STERILIZED JARS. MAKES APPROXIMATELY 4 LARGE JARS.

I'VE BEEN IN HOT WATER SO OFTEN, I FEEL LIKE A TEA BAG.

CORNED BEEF AND VEGGIES

THIS'LL WARM THE COCKLES O' YOUR IRISH HEART!

4 LBS. CORNED BEEF BRISKET	2 kg
12 OZ. BOTTLE OF BEER	341 mL
½ TBSP. WHOLE CLOVES	7 mL
SEVERAL PEPPERCORNS	
1 TBSP. BROWN SUGAR	15 mL
6-8 POTATOES, PEELED & CUT IN HALF	
1 STALK CELERY, CUT IN CHUNKS	
2 MEDIUM ONIONS, CUT IN QUARTERS	
6-8 CARROTS, CUT IN CHUNKS	
1 HEAD CABBAGE, CUT IN WEDGES	

USE NO LESS THAN A 4 LB. BRISKET. PUT IT IN A LARGE POT AND COVER WITH COLD WATER. ADD BEER, CLOVES, PEPPERCORNS AND BROWN SUGAR. SIMMER, COVERED, FOR 4½ HOURS. TO COOK VEGETABLES, REMOVE COOKED BRISKET FROM POT; KEEP WARM. TASTE BRISKET COOKING LIQUID; IF TOO SALTY, DISCARD ENOUGH LIQUID, REPLACING IT WITH FRESH WATER, TO REACH DESIRED SALT LEVEL. ADD POTATOES, CELERY, ONIONS AND CARROTS. HEAT TO BOILING. REDUCE HEAT, COVER AND SIMMER 15 MINUTES. SECURE CABBAGE WEDGES WITH TOOTHPICKS AND ADD TO OTHER VEGGIES. COOK 15 MINUTES LONGER OR UNTIL ALL VEGGIES ARE TENDER. DRAIN. ARRANGE VEGETABLES AROUND MEAT ON A PLATTER. BE SURE TO CARVE MEAT AGAINST THE GRAIN. SERVE WITH YOUR FAVORITE MUSTARD. SERVES 4-6.

VEAL 'N' VERMOUTH

A LIGHT DINNER FOR A SPECIAL EVENING

1½ LBS. VEAL SCALLOPINI	750 g
3-4 TBSP. FLOUR	45-60 mL
⅓ CUP BUTTER	75 mL
1 GARLIC CLOVE, MINCED	
1 SMALL ONION, CHOPPED	
1 SMALL RED PEPPER, SEEDED & CHOPPED	
1 SMALL YELLOW PEPPER, SEEDED & CHOPPED	
½ SMALL GREEN PEPPER, SEEDED & CHOPPED	
1 TBSP. LEMON JUICE	15 mL
2 CUPS SLICED MUSHROOMS	500 mL
½ CUP DRY VERMOUTH	125 mL

LIGHTLY FLOUR VEAL SLICES AND BROWN IN BUTTER. ADD GARLIC, ONION AND PEPPERS. SPRINKLE WITH LEMON JUICE. ADD MUSHROOMS AND VERMOUTH AND COVER. COOK OVER LOW HEAT FOR 25 MINUTES. SERVE WITH RICE AND BAKED ASPARAGUS ("GRAND SLAM" - PAGE 91). SERVES 4.

WHEN MY SHIP COMES IN, I'LL PROBABLY BE AT THE AIRPORT.

CHÂTEAUBRIAND WITH COGNAC SAUCE

IF YOU'RE GOING ALL OUT BUT WANT TO STAY IN . . .

2 BEEF TENDERLOINS, 2½ LBS. EACH	2 - 1.25 kg
5 MEDIUM GARLIC CLOVES, FINELY SLIVERED	
2½ TBSP. OLIVE OIL	37 mL

COGNAC MUSTARD SAUCE

1½ TBSP. BUTTER OR MARGARINE	22 mL
4 MEDIUM SHALLOTS, MINCED	
2 CUPS BEEF STOCK	500 mL
2 TBSP. COGNAC OR BRANDY	30 mL
2 TBSP. DIJON MUSTARD	30 mL
½ CUP BUTTER, CUT INTO 8 PIECES	125 mL
3 TBSP. CHOPPED, FRESH PARSLEY	45 mL
SALT & FRESHLY GROUND PEPPER TO TASTE	

CUT ¾" DEEP SLITS IN MEAT. INSERT GARLIC SLIVERS INTO SLITS. PREHEAT OVEN TO 450°F. IN LARGE SKILLET HEAT OIL AND BROWN MEAT ON ALL SIDES. PLACE MEAT ON A RACK IN ROASTING PAN. SET SKILLET ASIDE. ROAST MEAT TO DESIRED DONENESS, ABOUT 40 MINUTES FOR MEDIUM-RARE.

TO MAKE SAUCE: MELT 1½ TBSP. BUTTER IN RESERVED SKILLET. ADD SHALLOTS AND SAUTÉ UNTIL SOFTENED. STIR IN STOCK, SCRAPING UP BROWN BITS. BRING TO BOIL AND COOK UNTIL REDUCED BY HALF. ADD COGNAC AND BOIL ONE

CHÂTEAUBRIAND WITH COGNAC SAUCE

THIS RECIPE CONTINUED FROM PAGE 100.

MINUTE. REDUCE HEAT TO LOW. WHISK IN MUSTARD THEN BUTTER, ONE PIECE AT A TIME. COOK JUST UNTIL BUTTER IS MELTED. STIR IN PARSLEY. SEASON WITH SALT AND PEPPER.

CARVE MEAT IN ½" SLICES. SPOON SAUCE OVER AND SERVE IMMEDIATELY WITH A VARIETY OF FRESH GARDEN VEGETABLES AND YOUR BEST BEAUJOLAIS. SERVES 12.

MAJOR GREY'S MEAT LOAF

JOLLY GOOD!

2 LBS. GROUND BEEF	1 kg
SALT & PEPPER TO TASTE	
1-2 TSP. CURRY	5-10 mL
2 EGGS, BEATEN	
¼ CUP FINELY CHOPPED ONION	60 mL
2 LARGE APPLES, PEELED & CHOPPED	
½ CUP ORANGE JUICE	125 mL
⅓ CUP MANGO CHUTNEY	75 mL

MIX GROUND BEEF WITH ALL INGREDIENTS EXCEPT CHUTNEY. PLACE IN A 9" X 5" LOAF PAN AND BAKE AT 350°F FOR ONE HOUR. DRAIN. SPREAD CHUTNEY ON LOAF AND BAKE ANOTHER 20 MINUTES. GOOD HOT OR COLD.

CAESAR BURGERS

A BURGER ABOVE REPROACH.

1½ LBS. LEAN GROUND BEEF	750 g
¼ CUP FRESHLY GRATED PARMESAN CHEESE	60 mL
2 TBSP. LEMON JUICE	30 mL
1 TBSP. ANCHOVY PASTE	15 mL
1 TBSP. WORCESTERSHIRE SAUCE	15 mL
1 EGG, BEATEN	
¼ TSP. PEPPER	1 mL
2 TBSP. OLIVE OIL	30 mL
1 GARLIC CLOVE, MINCED	
KAISER BUNS, HALVED	
LETTUCE	

COMBINE BEEF, HALF OF THE PARMESAN CHEESE, LEMON JUICE, ANCHOVY PASTE, WORCESTERSHIRE SAUCE, EGG AND PEPPER. SHAPE INTO 4 PATTIES ABOUT ¾" THICK. BROIL GRILL. COMBINE OIL AND GARLIC, BRUSH OVER CUT SIDE OF BUNS. GRILL UNTIL TOASTED. SPRINKLE BURGERS WITH REMAINING CHEESE. TOP EACH WITH LETTUCE AND SERVE ON BUNS. SERVES 4.

THE BEST WAY TO KEEP YOUR DAUGHTER OUT OF HOT WATER IS TO PUT SOME DISHES IN IT.

PICTURED ON OVERLEAF

GRILLED HALIBUT AND
PEPPERS JULIENNE - PAGE 128

ORZO WITH PARMESAN AND BASIL
- PAGE 81

SLOPPY JOE POTATOES

MEAL ON A PEEL

3 LARGE BAKING POTATOES	
½ LB. LEAN GROUND BEEF	250 g
1 RED OR GREEN PEPPER, FINELY CHOPPED	
2 GREEN ONIONS, FINELY CHOPPED	
1 GARLIC CLOVE, CRUSHED	
14 OZ. CAN TOMATO SAUCE	398 mL
½ CUP CORN KERNELS, CANNED OR FROZEN	125 mL
1 TBSP. BROWN SUGAR	15 mL
1 TSP. CHILI POWDER	5 mL
½ TSP. OREGANO	2 mL
½ CUP WATER	125 mL
¼ CUP GRATED CHEDDAR CHEESE	60 mL

BAKE POTATOES. BROWN GROUND BEEF IN SKILLET. ADD REMAINING INGREDIENTS EXCEPT CHEESE. STIR AND SIMMER, UNCOVERED, FOR ABOUT 5 MINUTES. CUT POTATOES IN HALF, LENGTHWISE. LOOSEN POTATO AND GENEROUSLY SPOON MEAT MIXTURE OVER EACH POTATO HALF. SPRINKLE WITH CHEESE.

PLUMBER'S BUMPER STICKER: "IN OUR GAME, A FLUSH BEATS A FULL HOUSE."

TEX-MEX FAJITAS

OLÉ YOUSE GRINGOS!!

2 LBS. FLANK STEAK (1 LB. SERVES 3 PEOPLE) OR 3 CHICKEN BREASTS, SKINNED, BONED & HALVED	1 kg

MARINADE

½ CUP VEGETABLE OIL	125 mL
⅓ CUP LIME JUICE	75 mL
⅓ CUP RED WINE VINEGAR (ELIMINATE FOR CHICKEN)	75 mL
⅓ CUP CHOPPED ONION	75 mL
1 TSP. SUGAR	5 mL
1 TSP. OREGANO	5 mL
SALT & PEPPER TO TASTE	
¼ TSP. CUMIN	1 mL
2 GARLIC CLOVES, MINCED	
6 LARGE FLOUR TORTILLAS	

TOPPINGS

ONION SLICES, SAUTÉED
GREEN & RED PEPPER STRIPS, SAUTÉED
SHREDDED LETTUCE
GUACAMOLE, SOUR CREAM & SALSA

COMBINE MARINADE INGREDIENTS IN SHALLOW CASSEROLE. SCORE BOTH SIDES OF STEAK. ADD MEAT. COVER AND REFRIGERATE SEVERAL HOURS. REMOVE FROM MARINADE AND BARBECUE. SLICE

TEX-MEX FAJITAS

THIS RECIPE CONTINUED FROM PAGE 106.

IN THIN STRIPS ACROSS THE GRAIN. WRAP IN WARM TORTILLAS WITH ONIONS AND PEPPERS AND ANY OR ALL OF THE OTHER TOPPINGS.
SERVES 6 GRINGOS.

I ONCE MISSED A HOLE-IN-ONE BY ONLY FIVE STROKES.

GRILLED KOREAN SHORT RIBS

THE MARINADE ALSO WORKS WONDERS ON BABY BACK RIBS.

6 LARGE MEATY SHORT RIBS, TRIM FAT	
½ CUP DARK SOY SAUCE	125 mL
3 TBSP. VINEGAR	45 mL
2 TBSP. VEGETABLE OIL	30 mL
4 GARLIC CLOVES, CRUSHED	
2 GREEN ONIONS, FINELY CHOPPED	
1 TBSP. DRY MUSTARD	15 mL
1 TSP. GRATED FRESH GINGER	5 mL
FRESHLY GROUND PEPPER TO TASTE	

PARBOIL RIBS FOR 20 MINUTES. ARRANGE IN A SHALLOW PAN. COMBINE REMAINING INGREDIENTS, MIX WELL AND POUR OVER RIBS. MARINATE SEVERAL HOURS, TURNING FREQUENTLY. BARBECUE OR BROIL RIBS 3"-4" FROM HEAT, 5 MINUTES PER SIDE. SERVE WITH RICE, ASPARAGUS OR BROCCOLI. M-M-M-M GOOOOD!
SERVES 4.

OSSO BUCO MILANESE

CLASSIC ITALIAN FARE - A FLAVORFUL STEW MADE WITH VEAL SHANKS AND SERVED WITH RISOTTO (PAGE 82).

¼ CUP FLOUR	60 mL
SALT & FRESHLY GROUND PEPPER	
6 PIECES VEAL SHANK, ½ LB. EACH	6 - 250 g
⅓ CUP OLIVE OIL	75 mL
3 TBSP. BUTTER	45 mL
2 LARGE CARROTS, PEELED & SLICED	
1 LARGE ONION, DICED	
2 CELERY STALKS, SLICED	
1 TBSP. CHOPPED GARLIC	15 mL
2 BAY LEAVES, CRUSHED	
3 TBSP. CHOPPED FRESH MARJORAM OR 1 TBSP. DRIED	45 mL
3 TBSP. CHOPPED FRESH BASIL OR 1 TBSP. DRIED	45 mL
1 CUP CHOPPED FRESH PARSLEY	250 mL
GRATED RIND OF 1 LEMON	
1½ CUPS DRY WHITE WINE	375 mL
19 OZ. CAN ITALIAN PLUM TOMATOES, DRAINED & COARSELY CHOPPED	540 mL
1½ CUPS CHICKEN BROTH	375 mL

GREMOLATA FOR GARNISH

4 TSP. CHOPPED FRESH PARSLEY	20 mL
2 TSP. LEMON RIND	10 mL
1 GARLIC CLOVE, FINELY CHOPPED	

OSSO BUCO MILANESE

THIS RECIPE CONTINUED FROM PAGE 108

COMBINE FLOUR, SALT AND PEPPER IN A PLASTIC BAG. ADD VEAL SHANKS AND COAT WITH FLOUR MIXTURE. HEAT OIL IN A LARGE SKILLET AND BROWN VEAL ON BOTH SIDES. REMOVE VEAL FROM SKILLET, REDUCE HEAT AND ADD BUTTER, CARROTS, ONION, CELERY, GARLIC, BAY LEAVES, MARJORAM, BASIL, PARSLEY AND LEMON RIND. SAUTÉ FOR 5 MINUTES. ADD WINE AND CONTINUE COOKING FOR 5 MINUTES MORE. STIR IN TOMATOES AND BROTH. PLACE VEAL IN A CASSEROLE WITH THE SAUCE AND BAKE, COVERED, AT 325°F FOR 2 HOURS. GARNISH WITH GREMOLATA. SERVES 6.

GROUNDS FOR DIVORCE: FOR THEIR ANNIVERSARY SHE GAVE HIM A SET OF LUGGAGE - PACKED.

SZECHUAN BEEF WITH BROCCOLI

HERE'S A DELICIOUS WAY TO USE LEFTOVER RARE BEEF.

1 TBSP. CORNSTARCH	15 mL
3 TBSP. DRY SHERRY	45 mL
½ CUP OYSTER SAUCE	125 mL
¼ CUP WATER	60 mL
½ TSP. CRUSHED HOT RED PEPPER FLAKES	2 mL
2 TBSP. OIL	30 mL
1 TBSP. PEELED & SLIVERED GINGER	15 mL
1 GARLIC CLOVE, CRUSHED	
1 BUNCH BROCCOLI, CUT INTO FLORETS	
1 RED PEPPER, SEEDED & CUT INTO THIN STRIPS	
2 CELERY STALKS, CUT DIAGONALLY	
6 GREEN ONIONS, CUT INTO 1½" PIECES	
2 CUPS COOKED BEEF, CUT INTO STRIPS	500 mL

DISSOLVE CORNSTARCH IN SHERRY, OYSTER SAUCE AND WATER. ADD PEPPER FLAKES. IN A WOK OR LARGE SKILLET HEAT OIL OVER MEDIUM-HIGH HEAT. ADD GINGER AND GARLIC. STIR-FRY ONE MINUTE. ADD BROCCOLI, STIR-FRY 3 MINUTES. ADD RED PEPPER, CELERY AND GREEN ONIONS. STIR-FRY 3 MINUTES. ADD CORNSTARCH MIXTURE AND BEEF. STIR-FRY 3 MINUTES. SERVE WITH RICE. SERVES 4.

MY HUSBAND'S IDEA OF A SEVEN-COURSE DINNER IS A ROLL OF BOLOGNA AND A SIX-PACK.

ORANGE-ROSEMARY CHICKEN

SPLENDIFEROUS!

2 GARLIC CLOVES
1 ROASTING CHICKEN
1 ORANGE, QUARTERED
4 SPRIGS FRESH ROSEMARY OR
    1 TBSP. (15 mL) DRY
1 TBSP. OIL   15 mL
2 TBSP. ORANGE MARMALADE   30 mL
1 TBSP. CHOPPED FRESH ROSEMARY OR   15 mL
    1½ TSP. (7 mL) DRY

PREHEAT OVEN TO 325°F. PEEL GARLIC CLOVES AND PLACE IN CHICKEN CAVITY. STUFF UNPEELED ORANGE WEDGES INTO CAVITY ALONG WITH FRESH OR DRIED ROSEMARY. CLOSE THE CAVITY AND LOOSELY TIE LEGS TOGETHER. PLACE CHICKEN ON RACK IN ROASTING PAN. BRUSH SKIN WITH OIL. ROAST CHICKEN, UNCOVERED, FOR 2 HOURS, BASTING FREQUENTLY WITH THE PAN JUICES. MIX MARMALADE WITH ROSEMARY. BRUSH OVER CHICKEN AND CONTINUE ROASTING, BASTING WITH MIXTURE, ABOUT 10 MORE MINUTES. MAKE GRAVY WITH PAN DRIPPINGS AND SERVE WITH MASHED POTATOES.

NOTHING AGES YOUR CAR LIKE SOMEONE ELSE'S NEW ONE.

FRIED NOODLES SINGAPORE

MARINADE

1½ TSP. SESAME OIL	7 mL
3 TBSP. SOY SAUCE	45 mL
3 TBSP. CORN SYRUP	45 mL
1¼ CUPS WATER	300 mL
2 TBSP. SAKE OR SHERRY	30 mL
½ CUP CHOPPED ONION	125 mL
1½ TSP. GRATED FRESH GINGER	7 mL
¼-½ TSP. 5-SPICE POWDER	1-2 mL
⅛ TSP. TABASCO SAUCE	0.5 mL

2 CHICKEN BREASTS, SKINNED & BONED, CUT INTO STRIPS OR CUBES.

MAIN EVENT

10 OZ. RICE STICK NOODLES	285 g
¼ CUP OIL	60 mL
2 TSP. CURRY POWDER (MORE IF YOU LIKE IT HOT!)	10 mL
2 CUPS SHRIMP (OPTIONAL) PEELED & DEVEINED	500 mL
½ GREEN PEPPER, CUT IN STRIPS	
½ RED PEPPER, CUT IN STRIPS	
2 GREEN ONIONS, SLICED	
½ TSP. SUGAR	2 mL
1 TBSP. SOY SAUCE	15 mL

WHISK MARINADE INGREDIENTS TOGETHER. POUR OVER CHICKEN AND MARINATE FOR 4-6 HOURS.

COOK NOODLES ACCORDING TO PACKAGE DIRECTIONS. DRAIN IMMEDIATELY AND RUN UNDER COLD WATER.

FRIED NOODLES SINGAPORE

THIS RECIPE CONTINUED FROM PAGE 112.

HEAT HALF THE OIL IN A WOK OR LARGE SKILLET OVER HIGH HEAT. ADD NOODLES WITH ONE TSP. CURRY POWDER. STIR-FRY FOR 2-3 MINUTES. REMOVE NOODLES TO A HEATED DISH. HEAT REMAINING OIL. ADD SHRIMP, CHICKEN, PEPPERS, ONION AND ONE TSP. CURRY POWDER. STIR-FRY FOR 5 MINUTES. SPRINKLE WITH SUGAR AND SOY SAUCE AND STIR-FRY UNTIL SHRIMP IS PINK BUT THE CHICKEN ISN'T. RETURN NOODLES TO <u>PAN</u> AND LIGHTLY TOSS. SERVES 4 AS A MAIN COURSE, OR 6 IF SERVING WITH ANOTHER DISH.

HONEY-MUSTARD CHICKEN

YUMMY - MAKES LOTS OF SAUCE. GOOD WITH RICE.

3 LBS. CHICKEN PIECES	1.5 kg
½ CUP LIQUID HONEY	125 mL
¼ CUP BUTTER OR MARGARINE	60 mL
¼ CUP DIJON MUSTARD	60 mL
2-4 TSP. CURRY POWDER	10-20 mL
PINCH CAYENNE PEPPER	

PLACE CHICKEN IN SINGLE LAYER IN LARGE OVENPROOF DISH. COMBINE HONEY, BUTTER, MUSTARD, CURRY POWDER AND CAYENNE. POUR OVER CHICKEN. BAKE, UNCOVERED, AT 350°F FOR 20 MINUTES, BASTING ONCE. TURN PIECES OVER, BASTE AGAIN AND BAKE ANOTHER 20 MINUTES OR UNTIL PIECES ARE NO LONGER PINK INSIDE. SERVES 4-6.

CHICKEN BURRITOS

GUACAMOLE SAUCE

2 AVOCADOS	
JUICE OF ½ LEMON	
1 TBSP. CHILI POWDER	15 mL
¼ TSP. CAYENNE PEPPER	1 mL
1 TBSP. WORCESTERSHIRE SAUCE	15 mL
¼ TSP. GARLIC SALT (OR 1 FRESH	1 mL
CLOVE, MINCED)	
2 DROPS TABASCO SAUCE	

4 BONELESS CHICKEN BREASTS,	
SLICED IN THIN STRIPS	
1 TBSP. OLIVE OIL	15 mL
2 CUPS SOUR CREAM	500 mL
4 OZ. CAN CHOPPED GREEN CHILIES	114 mL
1 CUP GRATED MONTEREY JACK CHEESE	250 mL
1 CUP GRATED SHARP CHEDDAR CHEESE	250 mL
8 MEDIUM FLOUR TORTILLAS	
½ HEAD LETTUCE, SHREDDED	
2 TOMATOES, DICED	
4 GREEN ONIONS, CHOPPED	
RIPE OLIVES, SLICED	

COMBINE ALL GUACAMOLE INGREDIENTS AND MASH TOGETHER.

SAUTÉ CHICKEN IN OIL UNTIL JUST DONE. REMOVE FROM HEAT. ADD ONE CUP SOUR CREAM, CHILIES AND ½ CUP JACK CHEESE AND STIR TOGETHER. FILL TORTILLAS AND FOLD OVER BURRITO-STYLE. PLACE SIDE BY SIDE IN LIGHTLY GREASED CASSEROLE. SPRINKLE REMAINING

CHICKEN BURRITOS

THIS RECIPE CONTINUED FROM PAGE 114.

CHEESES ON TOP. BAKE AT 350°F FOR 20 MINUTES OR UNTIL CHEESE MELTS. REMOVE FROM OVEN AND TOP WITH GUACAMOLE SAUCE, REMAINING SOUR CREAM, LETTUCE, TOMATOES, ONIONS AND OLIVES.

CREDIT CARD: A LAMINATED LOAN SHARK.

STICKY BAKED CHICKEN

IF YOU HAVE TO LOOK GOOD IN AN HOUR . . .

SAUCE

1 CUP PEACH JAM	250 mL
½ CUP BARBECUE SAUCE	125 mL
½ CUP CHOPPED ONION	125 mL
2 TBSP. SOY SAUCE	30 mL

1 CHICKEN CUT INTO PIECES

COMBINE SAUCE INGREDIENTS IN SAUCEPAN AND HEAT UNTIL WELL-BLENDED. PLACE CHICKEN IN A SHALLOW 9" X 13" CASSEROLE AND POUR SAUCE OVER ALL. BAKE AT 325°F FOR ONE HOUR. BASTE DURING LAST ½ HOUR OF COOKING.

SOUTHWESTERN CHICKEN CHILI

2½ LBS. CHICKEN BREASTS	1.25 kg
2 TBSP. VEGETABLE OIL	30 mL
2 ONIONS, CHOPPED	
2 GARLIC CLOVES, MINCED	
3 TBSP. CHILI POWDER (USE ALL OF IT!)	45 mL
2 TSP. CUMIN	10 mL
1 TSP. OREGANO	5 mL
3 TBSP. CORIANDER	45 mL
SALT & PEPPER TO TASTE	
4 CARROTS, SLICED	
3 STALKS CELERY, CHOPPED	
28 OZ. CAN TOMATOES	796 mL
3 TBSP. TOMATO PASTE	45 mL
2 TBSP. LIME JUICE	30 mL
1 TSP. SUGAR	5 mL
12 OZ. CAN KERNEL CORN	341 mL
14 OZ. CAN KIDNEY BEANS	398 mL
14 OZ. CAN GARBANZO BEANS	398 mL
1 GREEN PEPPER, SEEDED & CHOPPED	

SKIN AND BONE CHICKEN. CUT INTO BITE-SIZED PIECES. IN A DUTCH OVEN, BROWN CHICKEN IN OIL. ADD ONIONS AND GARLIC AND SAUTÉ UNTIL ONIONS ARE SOFT. ADD CHILI, CUMIN, OREGANO, CORIANDER, SALT AND PEPPER. COOK AND STIR FOR 3 MINUTES. ADD CARROTS, CELERY, TOMATOES, TOMATO PASTE, LIME JUICE AND SUGAR TO CHICKEN MIXTURE. BRING TO BOIL, REDUCE TO SIMMER, COVER AND COOK FOR ONE HOUR. ADD CORN, KIDNEY AND GARBANZO BEANS AND GREEN PEPPER. SIMMER 30 MINUTES MORE.

SOUTHWESTERN CHICKEN CHILI

THIS RECIPE CONTINUED FROM PAGE 116.

SERVES MORE THAN 8 GOOD FRIENDS (OR 9 RELATIVES AND ONE AMAZED MOTHER-IN-LAW!). MAKE IT A MEAL WITH YUCATÁN SALAD (PAGE 58) AND CRUSTY ROLLS.

OVEN-FRIED CHICKEN

A PERFECT PICNIC "PACK ALONG".

SEASONED FLOUR

1½ CUPS FLOUR	375 mL
4 TSP. DRY MUSTARD	20 mL
1 TBSP. PAPRIKA	15 mL
SALT & PEPPER TO TASTE	
CHICKEN PIECES, AS NEEDED	
¼ CUP MARGARINE	60 mL

COMBINE SEASONED FLOUR INGREDIENTS AND STORE IN A JAR. PREHEAT OVEN TO 400°F. PLACE REQUIRED AMOUNT OF DRY MIXTURE IN A PAPER BAG, ADD CHICKEN AND SHAKE DEM BONES. MELT MARGARINE IN BAKING PAN. PLACE CHICKEN IN PAN AND BAKE 20 MINUTES. TURN AND BAKE ANOTHER 20 MINUTES, OR UNTIL GOLDEN BROWN. (SEE PICTURE - PAGE 53.)

MAPLE-ORANGE CHICKEN

1 ORANGE, ZEST AND JUICE
½ CUP MAPLE SYRUP   125 mL
½ TSP. NUTMEG   2 mL
½ TSP. GINGER OR 1 TBSP.   2 mL
        FRESH GINGER, CHOPPED
1 TBSP. OIL   15 mL
1 CHICKEN, CUT INTO PIECES
2 LARGE ONIONS, THINLY SLICED

COMBINE ORANGE ZEST, JUICE, MAPLE SYRUP,
NUTMEG, GINGER AND OIL. POUR OVER CHICKEN
PIECES AND MARINATE SEVERAL HOURS IN
REFRIGERATOR. LINE BOTTOM OF SHALLOW
BAKING DISH WITH ONIONS AND ARRANGE
CHICKEN PIECES ON TOP. BASTE WITH
RESERVED MARINADE. BAKE AT 350°F FOR ONE
HOUR. SERVES 4.

THERE'LL BE NO CANDLES ON HER BIRTHDAY
CAKE. SHE'S IN NO MOOD TO MAKE LIGHT OF
HER AGE.

LIME GRILLED CHICKEN

A LOW-CAL. CREATION TO BROIL OR GRILL. RUB HERBS BETWEEN YOUR HANDS TO RELEASE FLAVORS.

½ CUP FRESH LIME JUICE (2 LARGE LIMES)	125 mL
¼ CUP VEGETABLE OIL	60 mL
2 TBSP. HONEY	30 mL
1 TSP. THYME	5 mL
1 TSP. ROSEMARY	5 mL
1 GARLIC CLOVE, CRUSHED	
2 WHOLE CHICKEN BREASTS, SKINNED, BONED & HALVED	

IN A BOWL COMBINE ALL INGREDIENTS EXCEPT CHICKEN, WHISKING UNTIL WELL-BLENDED. MARINATE CHICKEN BREASTS IN LIME MIXTURE 1-2 HOURS. BROIL OR GRILL APPROXIMATELY 4 MINUTES PER SIDE UNTIL CHICKEN IS COOKED THROUGH. BASTE DURING COOKING. SERVES 4.

WHY IS THE PERSON WHO SNORES ALWAYS THE FIRST ONE TO FALL ASLEEP?

CHICKEN BREASTS STUFFED WITH ASPARAGUS

CELEBRATE THE RITES OF SPRING!

4 WHOLE CHICKEN BREASTS, HALVED, BONED & POUNDED	
24 MEDIUM ASPARAGUS SPEARS, LIGHTLY BLANCHED	
¼ CUP BUTTER, MELTED	60 mL
¼ CUP DIJON MUSTARD	60 mL
2 GARLIC CLOVES, FINELY CHOPPED	
¼ CUP WHITE WINE	60 mL
1½ CUPS BREAD CRUMBS	375 mL
1 TBSP. GRATED PARMESAN CHEESE	15 mL
2 TBSP. FINELY CHOPPED PARSLEY	30 mL

PREPARE CHICKEN AND ASPARAGUS. COMBINE THE BUTTER, MUSTARD, GARLIC AND WINE. DIP THE CHICKEN BREASTS IN THIS MIXTURE TO COAT THEM. PLACE 3 ASPARAGUS SPEARS ON EACH BREAST AND ROLL, SECURING WITH A TOOTHPICK. MIX BREAD CRUMBS, PARMESAN AND PARSLEY TOGETHER AND ROLL THE BREASTS IN THIS MIXTURE. BAKE 30 MINUTES AT 350°F. SERVES 4-6. PASS THE BLENDER HOLLANDAISE SAUCE (PAGE 92) AND HEAR THE RAVES. (SEE PICTURE - OPPOSITE.)

PEOPLE WILL BELIEVE ANYTHING IF YOU WHISPER IT.

PICTURED ON OVERLEAF

CHICKEN BREASTS STUFFED WITH
ASPARAGUS – PAGE 120

LEMON RICE – PAGE 80

PHEASANT MADEIRA

HAVE SOME MADEIRA, M' DEAR!

8 PHEASANT BREASTS, SKINLESS	
1 CUP CREAM	250 mL
½ CUP FLOUR	125 mL
½ TSP. SALT	2 mL
½ TSP. PAPRIKA	2 mL
½ CUP BUTTER	125 mL
1 CUP MADEIRA WINE	250 mL
1 CUP SLICED GREEN GRAPES	250 mL

DIP BREASTS IN ½ CUP CREAM, THEN DREDGE IN COMBINED FLOUR, SALT AND PAPRIKA. SAUTÉ LIGHTLY IN BUTTER. REMOVE BREASTS. SET ASIDE. ADD MADEIRA AND COOK FOR A FEW MINUTES, SCRAPING BITS FROM BOTTOM OF PAN. STIR IN ½ CUP CREAM. REHEAT AND PLACE BREASTS BACK IN SAUCE. COOK ANOTHER 20 MINUTES (LESS IF BREASTS ARE SMALL). ADD GRAPES JUST BEFORE SERVING. GREAT WITH WILD RICE. SERVES 4.

WE'VE BEEN THROUGH A LOT TOGETHER - AND MOST OF IT IS YOUR FAULT.

BAKED SNAPPER ITALIANO

RED SNAPPER FOR 6
MILK TO MARINATE

SEASONED FLOUR

2/3 CUP PARMESAN CHEESE	150	mL
1 1/4 CUPS FLOUR	300	mL
1 TSP. ITALIAN SEASONING	5	mL
1 TBSP. PAPRIKA	15	mL
1 TSP. ONION POWDER	5	mL
1 TSP. BLACK PEPPER	5	mL
1/2 TSP. BAKING POWDER	2	mL
1/4 TSP. GARLIC POWDER	1	mL
1 1/2 TSP. SALT	7	mL
1/2 CUP BUTTER, MELTED	125	mL

MARINATE FISH FILLETS OVERNIGHT IN MILK.
REMOVE EACH FILLET AND DREDGE IN
SEASONED FLOUR. DRIZZLE WITH BUTTER. BAKE
AT 400°F FOR ABOUT 20 MINUTES.

"I HEARD SHE HAD AN AFFAIR."
"OH, WHO CATERED IT?"

WILD WEST SALMON

SCRUMPTIOUS COMPANY FARE FOR THE BARBECUE SEASON

1 WHOLE SALMON, BUTTERFLIED (SEE METHOD)

MARINADE

1 TBSP. BROWN SUGAR	15 mL
½ CUP RYE WHISKEY	125 mL
1 TBSP. MOLASSES	15 mL
½ CUP VEGETABLE OIL	125 mL
2 TBSP. SOY SAUCE	30 mL
1 TBSP. EACH SALT & PEPPER	15 mL
2 GARLIC CLOVES, MINCED	

TO PREPARE SALMON: REMOVE HEAD, TAIL AND FINS FROM SALMON. RUN A SHARP KNIFE DOWN BACKBONE UNTIL SALMON OPENS FLAT. REMOVE BACKBONE. PLACE FLESH SIDE DOWN IN A LARGE DISH.

COMBINE MARINADE INGREDIENTS, MIX WELL AND POUR OVER SALMON. MARINATE OVERNIGHT IN REFRIGERATOR.

WHEN READY TO GRILL, REMOVE SALMON FROM MARINADE AND PLACE SKIN SIDE DOWN ON HEAVY FOIL. BARBECUE UNTIL FLESH IS OPAQUE AND FLAKES EASILY, 20-30 MINUTES. SERVE WITH PAPAYA AVOCADO SALAD (PAGE 51) OR DOUBLE GREEN SALAD (PAGE 52) AND CRUSTY ROLLS. YOU'LL HAVE AN "ACES" EVENING.

ORANGE ROUGHY DIJONNAISE

SAUCE

2 TBSP. BUTTER OR MARGARINE	30 mL
1 SMALL ONION, CHOPPED	
2 TBSP. FLOUR	30 mL
1/3 CUP DRY WHITE WINE	75 mL
1/4 CUP WATER	60 mL
SALT & PEPPER TO TASTE	
1 TBSP. DIJON MUSTARD	15 mL
1/3 CUP MILK OR LIGHT CREAM	75 mL
1/3 CUP GRATED MOZZARELLA CHEESE	75 mL
1 LARGE TOMATO, CHOPPED	
2 LBS. ORANGE ROUGHY FILLETS	1 kg
2 TBSP. BUTTER OR MARGARINE, MELTED	30 mL
2 TBSP. FRESH LEMON JUICE	30 mL
SALT & FRESHLY GROUND PEPPER TO TASTE	

TO MAKE SAUCE: MELT BUTTER IN SAUCEPAN, SAUTÉ ONION UNTIL SOFT. ADD FLOUR AND COOK 2 MINUTES. ADD WINE, WATER, SALT, PEPPER AND MUSTARD. STIR AND COOK UNTIL THICKENED. ADD MILK AND CHEESE. WHEN CHEESE MELTS, ADD TOMATO. REMOVE FROM HEAT. COVER AND KEEP WARM.

TO PREPARE FISH: ARRANGE FILLETS ON GREASED BROILER PAN, TURNING UNDER THIN ENDS. BRUSH WITH MELTED BUTTER, SPRINKLE WITH LEMON, SALT AND PEPPER. BROIL 8-10 MINUTES, UNTIL FISH FLAKES WITH A FORK. REMOVE TO OVENPROOF SERVING DISH. COVER FILLETS WITH SAUCE. RETURN TO BROILER UNTIL SAUCE IS LIGHTLY BROWNED. SERVES 6.

ORANGE-GINGER HALIBUT

4 HALIBUT STEAKS	
2 TBSP. MARGARINE, MELTED	30 mL
SALT & PEPPER TO TASTE	
2 TSP. CORNSTARCH	10 mL
1 TSP. GRATED FRESH GINGER	5 mL
½ TSP. CHICKEN BOUILLON POWDER	2 mL
¾ CUP ORANGE JUICE	175 mL
1 TBSP. SOY SAUCE	15 mL
1 GREEN ONION, FINELY CHOPPED	

GREASE BROILING PAN. PLACE FISH IN A SINGLE LAYER ON RACK. BRUSH FISH WITH ONE TBSP. MELTED MARGARINE AND SPRINKLE WITH SALT AND PEPPER. BROIL 4" FROM HEAT FOR 5 MINUTES. TURN FISH OVER, BRUSH WITH ONE TBSP. MELTED MARGARINE AND BROIL 5 MORE MINUTES, OR UNTIL FISH FLAKES EASILY.

WHILE FISH IS COOKING, COMBINE CORNSTARCH, GINGER AND BOUILLON IN A SMALL SAUCEPAN. STIR IN ORANGE JUICE AND SOY SAUCE AND COOK OVER MEDIUM HEAT UNTIL THICK AND BUBBLY, ABOUT ONE MINUTE. ADD ONION AND SIMMER OVER LOW HEAT UNTIL FISH IS COOKED. PLACE FISH ON WARMED PLATES AND SPOON SAUCE ON FISH. SERVE WITH LEMON RICE (PAGE 80), PEA PODS AND BUTTERED CARROTS SPRINKLED WITH GINGER AND LEMON JUICE.

GRILLED HALIBUT AND PEPPERS JULIENNE

A POTPOURRI OF PEPPERS - THE PERFECT PARTNER FOR YOUR FAVORITE FISH. SERVE WITH ORZO WITH PARMESAN AND BASIL (PAGE 81).

1 RED PEPPER	
1 GREEN PEPPER	
1 YELLOW PEPPER	
1 ONION	
2 STALKS CELERY	
1 TOMATO	
2 TBSP. BUTTER OR MARGARINE	30 mL
1 TSP. CHOPPED FRESH PARSLEY	5 mL
A GENEROUS SPRINKLE OF: PAPRIKA, CURRY POWDER & CAYENNE	
SALT & PEPPER TO TASTE	
2/3 CUP WHITE WINE	150 mL
4 HALIBUT STEAKS	
SPRINKLING OF PAPRIKA & PEPPER	

CUT PEPPERS (REMOVE SEEDS), ONION AND CELERY INTO THIN STRIPS. COARSELY CHOP THE TOMATO. MELT BUTTER IN SKILLET. ADD PREPARED VEGGIES AND ALL REMAINING INGREDIENTS, EXCEPT THE FISH. SIMMER 5 MINUTES. WHILE VEGGIES ARE COOKING, PREPARE AND COOK FISH. BRUSH WITH OIL AND SPRINKLE WITH PAPRIKA AND PEPPER. GRILL UNTIL FISH IS OPAQUE AND FLAKES EASILY, ABOUT 4 MINUTES EACH SIDE. SPOON SIMMERED VEGGIES AND PAN JUICES OVER FISH. GOOD FOR YOUR BOD AND GREAT FOR YOUR CULINARY REPUTATION!!
ENOUGH FOR 4. (SEE PICTURE - PAGE 103.)

CIOPPINO

AN EASY ONE-POT FEAST! A FISHERMAN'S STEW.

1 LARGE ONION, CHOPPED	
1 RED PEPPER, CHOPPED	
1 CUP SLICED CELERY	250 mL
3-4 GARLIC CLOVES, MINCED	
¼ CUP OLIVE OIL	60 mL
2 - 28 OZ. CANS ROMA TOMATOES	2 - 796 mL
2 CUPS FISH STOCK OR WATER	500 mL
1 CUP DRY WHITE WINE	250 mL
2 BAY LEAVES	
2 TSP. BASIL	10 mL
1 TSP. OREGANO	5 mL
½ TSP. CRUSHED HOT RED PEPPER FLAKES	2 mL
2 TBSP. CHOPPED FRESH PARSLEY	30 mL
SALT & PEPPER TO TASTE	
1 LB. WHITE FISH, CUT INTO CHUNKS	500 g
1 LB. MEDIUM SHRIMP, PEELED	500 g
½ LB. FRESH SCALLOPS	250 g
1 LB. FRESH MUSSELS, IN SHELLS	500 g
1 LB. FRESH CLAMS, IN SHELLS	500 g

IN A LARGE POT, SAUTÉ ONION, RED PEPPER, CELERY AND GARLIC IN OIL UNTIL SOFT. ADD TOMATOES, FISH STOCK OR WATER, WINE AND SEASONINGS. SIMMER FOR 45 MINUTES, STIRRING OCCASIONALLY TO BREAK UP TOMATOES. ADD FISH, SHRIMP AND SCALLOPS. SIMMER FOR 10 MINUTES MORE. ADD MUSSELS AND CLAMS AND SIMMER FOR ANOTHER 5 MINUTES. (DISCARD ANY SHELLS THAT DO NOT OPEN.) LADLE INTO SHALLOW BOWLS AND SERVE WITH FRESH CRUSTY BREAD FOR DIPPING. SERVES 4-6.

SHRIMP AND SCALLOP SUPREME

2 TBSP. OLIVE OIL	30 mL
1 ONION, CHOPPED	
3 GARLIC CLOVES, MINCED	
2-28 OZ. CANS TOMATOES, PURÉED WITH JUICE	2 - 796 mL
1 LB. SHRIMP, DEVEINED & BUTTERFLIED	500 g
3/4 LB. SCALLOPS, HALVED IF LARGE	340 g
1 CUP FROZEN PEAS, THAWED	250 mL
1/4 CUP CHOPPED FRESH PARSLEY	60 mL
1 TSP. SALT	5 mL
1/2 TSP. PEPPER	2 mL
3 CUPS COOKED LONG-GRAIN RICE	750 mL

TOPPING

1/3 CUP BUTTER	75 mL
2 GARLIC CLOVES, MINCED	
2 CUPS FRESH BREAD CRUMBS	500 mL

IN DUTCH OVEN HEAT OIL OVER MEDIUM HEAT. COOK ONION AND GARLIC FOR 5 MINUTES. ADD TOMATOES, COOK 15 MINUTES. ADD SEAFOOD, COOK 5 MINUTES. STIR IN PEAS, PARSLEY, SALT AND PEPPER. SEASON RICE WITH SALT AND PEPPER TO TASTE AND SPREAD IN GREASED GLASS 9" X 13" PAN. SPREAD SEAFOOD MIXTURE OVER RICE.

TO MAKE TOPPING: SAUTÉ GARLIC IN BUTTER. ADD BREAD CRUMBS AND SEASON WITH SALT AND PEPPER. SPRINKLE OVER CASSEROLE. MAY BE REFRIGERATED AT THIS POINT FOR UP TO 24

SHRIMP AND SCALLOP SUPREME

THIS RECIPE CONTINUED FROM PAGE 130.

HOURS. REMOVE FROM REFRIGERATOR ½ HOUR BEFORE BAKING. BAKE AT 350°F FOR 30-40 MINUTES, OR UNTIL BUBBLING AND TOP IS BROWNED AND CRISP. DO NOT OVERCOOK. SERVE WITH ASPARAGUS AND WARM ROLLS. SERVES 8-10.

TWO CAN LIVE AS CHEAPLY AS ONE - IF ONE DOESN'T SHOW UP.

SCALLOPS PAPRIKA

3 TBSP. BUTTER	45 mL
1 LB. SCALLOPS	500 g
3 TBSP. FLOUR	45 mL
1 CUP WHIPPING CREAM	250 mL
¼ CUP SHERRY	60 mL
1 TBSP. PAPRIKA	15 mL
3 GREEN ONIONS, THINLY SLICED	

HEAT THE BUTTER IN A LARGE HEAVY SKILLET. ADD SCALLOPS AND SAUTÉ FOR 5 MINUTES. SPRINKLE IN THE FLOUR. COOK 2 MINUTES. ADD WHIPPING CREAM, SHERRY AND PAPRIKA. REDUCE HEAT AND SIMMER 8-10 MINUTES OR UNTIL THICKENED. SPRINKLE WITH GREEN ONIONS. SERVE OVER RICE OR NOODLES. SERVES 4.

SHRIMP STIR-FRY

2 TBSP. SESAME OIL	30 mL
1 GARLIC CLOVE, MINCED	
½ TSP. MINCED FRESH GINGER	2 mL
24-36 PEELED SHRIMP	
A HANDFUL OF SNOW PEAS	
2 CUPS BROCCOLI FLORETS	500 mL
2 STALKS CELERY, SLICED DIAGONALLY	
1 SMALL WHITE ONION, SLIVERED	
1 RED BELL PEPPER, SLICED	
2 CUPS FRESH BEAN SPROUTS	500 mL
½ CUP OYSTER SAUCE	125 mL
1 TBSP. SOY SAUCE	15 mL
1 TBSP. LIQUID HONEY	15 mL
¼ CUP WHITE WINE	60 mL

HEAT SESAME OIL IN WOK OR SKILLET OVER MEDIUM HEAT. SAUTÉ GARLIC AND GINGER FOR 30 SECONDS. ADD SHRIMP AND COOK 30 SECONDS. ADD VEGGIES AND STIR-FRY UNTIL TENDER CRISP - ABOUT 3 MINUTES. STIR IN OYSTER SAUCE, SOY SAUCE, HONEY AND WINE. TOSS TOGETHER FOR 2 MINUTES. SERVE WITH RICE. SERVES 4.

NO MATTER WHAT HAPPENS- THERE'S ALWAYS SOMEONE WHO KNEW IT WOULD.

SZECHUAN SHRIMP

2 TBSP. OIL	30 mL
1 LB. LARGE RAW SHRIMP, PEELED	500 g
¼ CUP CHOPPED GREEN ONION	60 mL
2 TBSP. MINCED FRESH GINGER	30 mL
3 GARLIC CLOVES, MINCED	
2 TBSP. SHERRY	30 mL
2 TBSP. SOY SAUCE	30 mL
2 TBSP. KETCHUP	30 mL
2 TBSP. CHILI SAUCE	30 mL
1 TSP. HOT RED PEPPER FLAKES	5 mL

HEAT OIL IN WOK OR SKILLET. ADD SHRIMP, ONION, GINGER AND GARLIC. STIR-FRY UNTIL SHRIMP (IS) "WHERE'S OUR ENGLISH MAJOR?" (ARE) PINK. BLEND IN SHERRY AND SOY SAUCE. ADD REMAINING INGREDIENTS AND STIR WELL. SERVE WITH RICE AND SNOW PEAS. SERVES 4.

SIGN IN A SUPERMARKET: EXPRESS LANE - $200.00 OR LESS.

CRUNCHY OVEN-BAKED FISH

1 LB. FISH FILLETS	500 g
1/3 CUP SOUR CREAM	75 mL
1 TBSP. LEMON JUICE	15 mL
1/2 TSP. CHILI POWDER	2 mL
3/4 CUP CRUSHED CORN CHIPS	175 mL
2 TBSP. MARGARINE, MELTED	30 mL

CUT FISH INTO SERVING PIECES. MIX SOUR CREAM, LEMON JUICE AND CHILI POWDER TOGETHER. DIP FISH PIECES INTO MIXTURE AND COAT WITH CORN CHIPS. PLACE FISH IN A GREASED 9" X 13" BAKING DISH AND DRIZZLE WITH MELTED MARGARINE. BAKE, UNCOVERED, AT 425°F FOR 10-12 MINUTES. SERVE WITH PICANTE SALSA (PAGE 37). SERVES 4.

WHEN YOU'RE IN DEEP WATER, IT'S A GOOD IDEA TO KEEP YOUR MOUTH SHUT.

PORK LOIN ROAST

YOU NEED A ZINGER - AND THIS IS IT!!! SURE TO BECOME A FAVORITE.

4-6 LBS. BONELESS PORK LOIN ROAST	2-2.5 kg

SAUCE

1 CUP PLUM JAM	250 mL
1/3 CUP ORANGE JUICE CONCENTRATE, THAWED	75 mL
1/3 CUP PINEAPPLE JUICE	75 mL
1/4 CUP SOY SAUCE	60 mL
1 TSP. ONION POWDER	5 mL
1/4 TSP. GARLIC POWDER	1 mL

PREHEAT OVEN TO 350°F. LINE ROASTING PAN WITH FOIL. COOK ROAST UNTIL TEMPERATURE ON MEAT THERMOMETER REACHES 170°F (30 MINUTES PER POUND). COMBINE SAUCE INGREDIENTS IN A SMALL SAUCEPAN AND SIMMER FOR 5 MINUTES. AFTER ROAST REACHES 170°F, BRUSH FREQUENTLY WITH SAUCE WHILE CONTINUING TO ROAST FOR A FURTHER 30 MINUTES. PASS REMAINING SAUCE WITH ROAST. SERVE WITH ROASTED NEW POTATOES WITH HERBS (PAGE 77), THE CARROT PATCH (PAGE 84) AND SAUCY BRUSSELS SPROUTS (PAGE 88). SERVES 6.

KNOW-IT-ALL - A HAIRDRESSER WHO MOONLIGHTS AS A CAB DRIVER.

LAMB CURRY

THE BEST PART ABOUT EATING A CURRY IS THE CONDIMENTS YOU GET TO ADD AT THE TABLE - SORT OF A DESIGNER DINNER.

2 TBSP. CURRY POWDER OR TO TASTE	30 mL
½ TSP. EACH: GINGER, TURMERIC, PAPRIKA, SALT, PEPPER	2 mL
¼ TSP. CAYENNE PEPPER	1 mL
2½ LBS. BONED LAMB SHANK CUT IN ¾" CUBES	1.25 kg
3 TBSP. BUTTER OR MARGARINE	45 mL
2 ONIONS, CHOPPED	
2 STALKS CELERY, CHOPPED	
1 GREEN PEPPER, SEEDED & CHOPPED	
1-2 GARLIC CLOVES, MINCED	
2 APPLES, PEELED & CHOPPED	
½ CUP RAISINS	125 mL
2 TBSP. FLOUR	30 mL
1 CUP CHICKEN BROTH	250 mL
1 CUP COCONUT MILK	250 mL
¼ CUP MANGO CHUTNEY	60 mL
SALT TO TASTE	
⅓ CUP YOGURT	75 mL

CONDIMENTS

SMALL BOWLS OF CHUTNEY, TOASTED COCONUT, MANDARIN ORANGE SECTIONS, CHOPPED GREEN ONIONS AND PEANUTS. PASS THE HOT RED PEPPER FLAKES.

COMBINE SEASONINGS AND SET ASIDE. IN A SKILLET, SAUTÉ LAMB IN A SMALL AMOUNT OF BUTTER UNTIL BROWN. SET ASIDE IN A LARGE POT OR DUTCH OVEN. REMOVE EXCESS FAT FROM SKILLET, ADD REMAINING OF BUTTER AND

LAMB CURRY

THIS RECIPE CONTINUED FROM PAGE 136.

SAUTÉ ONION, CELERY, GREEN PEPPER AND GARLIC. SPRINKLE WITH HALF THE CURRY MIXTURE AND COOK BRIEFLY. ADD APPLES AND RAISINS, SPRINKLE WITH FLOUR AND STIR IN CHICKEN BROTH. ADD THIS MIXTURE TO MEAT IN THE DUTCH OVEN. ADD COCONUT MILK, THEN STIR IN THE REST OF THE CURRY MIXTURE, MANGO CHUTNEY AND SALT TO TASTE. SIMMER FOR AT LEAST ONE HOUR. HALF AN HOUR BEFORE SERVING, STIR IN YOGURT AND HEAT GENTLY TO SERVING TEMPERATURE. SERVE WITH RICE AND PASS THE CONDIMENTS. SERVES 6.

RACK OF LAMB WITH MUSTARD COATING

⅓ CUP FINE DRY BREAD CRUMBS	75 mL
1 LARGE GARLIC CLOVE, MINCED	
½ TSP. DRIED THYME	2 mL
¼ TSP. PEPPER	1 mL
4 TBSP. DIJON MUSTARD	60 mL
1 RACK OF LAMB	

COMBINE CRUMBS, GARLIC, THYME AND PEPPER. STIR IN 3 TBSP. MUSTARD. TRIM EXCESS FAT FROM MEAT. BRUSH REMAINING MUSTARD OVER FAT SIDE OF RACK. COAT WITH CRUMB MIXTURE AND BAKE AT 400°F FOR 20-30 MINUTES, UNTIL DONE AS DESIRED.

MEDALLIONS OF PORK

3 PORK TENDERLOINS	
2 TSP. DRY MUSTARD	10 mL
1 TSP. SALT	5 mL
1/4 TSP. FRESHLY GROUND PEPPER	1 mL
2 TBSP. BUTTER	30 mL
2-3 GARLIC CLOVES, MINCED	
1/2 CUP DRY VERMOUTH	125 mL
1/2 CUP WHITE WINE	125 mL
3/4-1 CUP ORANGE JUICE	175-250 mL
1 TBSP. FLOUR	15 mL
2 TBSP. WATER	30 mL
MINCED PARSLEY	
ORANGE ZEST	
ORANGE SLICES	

TRIM FAT AND SINEW FROM LOINS AND CUT IN 1/2" THICK SLICES. COMBINE DRY MUSTARD, SALT AND PEPPER AND LIGHTLY RUB INTO MEAT. IN A LARGE, HEAVY SKILLET, MELT BUTTER OVER MEDIUM-HIGH HEAT AND ADD PORK SLICES AND GARLIC. BROWN FOR 3-5 MINUTES ON EACH SIDE. ADD THE VERMOUTH, WINE AND ORANGE JUICE AND REDUCE HEAT. SIMMER, COVERED, FOR 8-10 MINUTES OR UNTIL MEAT IS TENDER. REMOVE THE MEDALLIONS TO A WARM PLATE AND COVER.

MAKE A PASTE OF THE FLOUR AND WATER. USING A WHISK, STIR THE PASTE INTO THE PAN JUICES AND SIMMER TO THICKEN. WHEN READY TO SERVE, RETURN THE MEDALLIONS TO THE HOT

THIS RECIPE IS CONTINUED ON PAGE 141.

PICTURED ON OVERLEAF

RED AND WHITE TORTELLINI
— PAGE 144

MEDALLIONS OF PORK

RECIPE CONTINUED FROM PAGE 138.

PAN GRAVY FOR A MINUTE. ARRANGE ON A WARMED SERVING PLATTER AND COVER WITH THE GRAVY. SPRINKLE WITH PARSLEY AND ORANGE ZEST. PLACE SPRIGS OF PARSLEY AND SLICES OF ORANGE AROUND THE PLATTER. SERVES 8.

A FOOL AND HIS MONEY ARE SOON PARTED – THE REST OF US WAIT TO BE TAXED.

NO-BRAINER KABOBS

THE TITLE SAYS IT ALL.

PORK TENDERLOIN OR CHICKEN, CUBED
        (ENOUGH FOR YOUR CROWD)
PEPPERS (RED, YELLOW, GREEN)
        CUT IN CHUNKS
ZUCCHINI, CUT IN CHUNKS
ONIONS, CUT IN WEDGES
MUSHROOMS
8 OZ. BOTTLE ITALIAN DRESSING   250 mL

PREPARE MEAT AND MARINATE IN ITALIAN DRESSING FOR SEVERAL HOURS. ALTERNATE VEGETABLES AND MEAT ON SKEWERS. BRUSH WITH DRESSING. BARBECUE OR BROIL UNTIL MEAT IS COOKED. SERVE WITH RICE OR PASTA.

CROWN ROAST OF PORK
WITH APPLE RAISIN STUFFING

1 CROWN ROAST OF PORK - 2 RIBS PER SERVING

STUFFING

1 CUP SEEDLESS RAISINS	250 mL
1 CUP CHOPPED ONION	250 mL
3 CUPS PEELED & CUBED APPLES	750 mL
7 CUPS SOFT BREAD CUBES	1.75 L
¾ CUP BUTTER OR MARGARINE, MELTED	175 mL
1½ TSP. SALT	7 mL
¼ TSP. PEPPER	1 mL
½ CUP FINELY CHOPPED PARSLEY	125 mL
1 GARLIC CLOVE, FINELY CHOPPED	
½ TSP. EACH: MACE, SAGE, NUTMEG & CLOVES	2 mL

PARBOIL RAISINS, DRAIN AND DRY. MIX STUFFING INGREDIENTS THOROUGHLY. PROTECT ENDS OF BONES ON ROAST WITH FOIL. FILL CAVITY OF THE ROAST WITH LARGE FOIL BALL. HEAT OVEN TO 450°F. PUT IN ROAST AND IMMEDIATELY TURN DOWN TO 350°F. COOK 30-45 MINUTES PER POUND. REMOVE FOIL BALL. PLACE STUFFING IN CENTER ONE HOUR BEFORE IT'S DONE. REMOVE FOIL AND ADD FRILLS TO THE ENDS OF BONES. PRETTY AS A PICTURE!

ANY HOUSEHOLD TASK IS FASCINATING TO A CHILD - UNTIL HE'S OLD ENOUGH TO DO IT.

ARTICHOKE SAUCE FOR PASTA

2 – 6 OZ. JARS MARINATED ARTICHOKE HEARTS	2 – 170 mL
1 TBSP. BUTTER	15 mL
1 CUP SLICED ONIONS	250 mL
2 TSP. DRIED BASIL	10 mL
½ CUP SOUR CREAM	125 mL
½ CUP RICOTTA CHEESE OR COTTAGE CHEESE	125 mL
CAYENNE PEPPER TO TASTE	
SALT & PEPPER TO TASTE	
PARMESAN CHEESE TO SPRINKLE	

COOKED PASTA FOR FOUR (FUSILLI IS A GOOD CHOICE)

DRAIN ARTICHOKE LIQUID INTO SKILLET. SLICE ARTICHOKE HEARTS INTO BITE-SIZED PIECES AND RESERVE. ADD BUTTER TO LIQUID, HEAT TO MEDIUM-HIGH, ADD ONIONS AND SAUTÉ UNTIL SOFT. ADD ARTICHOKE HEARTS AND BASIL AND COOK FOR 5 MINUTES. REDUCE HEAT, ADD SOUR CREAM, RICOTTA CHEESE, CAYENNE PEPPER, SALT AND PEPPER AND STIR UNTIL HEATED THROUGH. DON'T BOIL. TOSS WITH PASTA AND SPRINKLE WITH PARMESAN CHEESE. SERVES 4.

THE FUNNY THING ABOUT TROUBLE IS THAT IT ALWAYS STARTS OUT BEING FUN.

RED AND WHITE TORTELLINI

TORTELLINI IN TWO SAUCES.

TOMATO SAUCE

1 TBSP. BUTTER	15 mL
2 GARLIC CLOVES, MINCED	
1/4 CUP CHOPPED ONION	60 mL
14 OZ. CAN TOMATO SAUCE	398 mL
12 OZ. TORTELLINI, FRESH OR FROZEN	340 g

MUSHROOM PARMESAN SAUCE

2 TBSP. BUTTER	30 mL
2 CUPS SLICED FRESH MUSHROOMS	500 mL
1/4 CUP CHOPPED GREEN ONION	60 mL
2 TBSP. FLOUR	30 mL
2 CUPS MILK	500 mL
2/3 CUP GRATED PARMESAN CHEESE	150 mL
SALT & PEPPER	
1 1/2 CUPS GRATED MOZZARELLA CHEESE	375 mL
GRATED PARMESAN CHEESE	

TO MAKE TOMATO SAUCE: MELT BUTTER AND SAUTÉ GARLIC AND ONION UNTIL TENDER. ADD TOMATO SAUCE AND BRING TO BOIL. REDUCE HEAT, COVER AND SIMMER 10 MINUTES.

COOK TORTELLINI ACCORDING TO PACKAGE DIRECTIONS.

TO MAKE MUSHROOM SAUCE: MELT BUTTER AND SAUTÉ MUSHROOMS AND GREEN ONION UNTIL TENDER. SPRINKLE WITH FLOUR, AND GRADUALLY

RED AND WHITE TORTELLINI

THIS RECIPE CONTINUED FROM PAGE 144.

STIR IN MILK. COOK AND STIR OVER MEDIUM HEAT UNTIL MIXTURE THICKENS TO CONSISTENCY OF MUSHROOM SOUP. REMOVE FROM HEAT. STIR IN PARMESAN CHEESE, SALT AND PEPPER TO TASTE. ADD MUSHROOM PARMESAN SAUCE TO COOKED, DRAINED TORTELLINI.

TO SERVE: SPREAD TOMATO SAUCE OVER BOTTOM OF A LARGE SHALLOW CASSEROLE. SPOON TORTELLINI MUSHROOM MIXTURE ON TOP LEAVING A RED BORDER OF TOMATO SAUCE. SPRINKLE WITH MOZZARELLA CHEESE AND ADDITIONAL PARMESAN CHEESE. PLACE UNDER BROILER UNTIL CHEESE IS MELTED AND GOLDEN. SERVE IMMEDIATELY. SERVES 4-6.

(SEE PICTURE - PAGE 139.)

I WAS TRYING TO GET A NEW CAR FOR MY WIFE, BUT NO ONE WOULD SWAP.

PESTO LASAGNE

RICH, RICH, RICH!

TOMATO SAUCE

4 GARLIC CLOVES, MINCED	
2 ONIONS, CHOPPED	
⅓ CUP OLIVE OIL	75 mL
28 OZ. CAN CRUSHED TOMATOES	796 mL
SALT TO TASTE	

PESTO

1 CUP FRESH BASIL	250 mL
½ CUP PINE NUTS	125 mL
⅓ CUP GRATED PARMESAN	75 mL
⅓ CUP OLIVE OIL	75 mL

BÉCHAMEL SAUCE

3 TBSP. BUTTER	45 mL
¼ CUP FLOUR	60 mL
¼ TSP. NUTMEG	1 mL
SALT & PEPPER TO TASTE	
2 CUPS MILK	500 mL

8-10 LASAGNA NOODLES	
1 LB. BOCCONCINI OR MOZZARELLA, SLICED	500 g
½ CUP GRATED PARMESAN	125 mL

TO MAKE TOMATO SAUCE: SAUTÉ GARLIC AND ONION IN OIL UNTIL TRANSPARENT. ADD TOMATOES AND SALT. COOK UNTIL THICKENED. SET ASIDE.

TO MAKE PESTO: PURÉE ALL INGREDIENTS IN

PESTO LASAGNE

THIS RECIPE CONTINUED FROM PAGE 146.

FOOD PROCESSOR. SET ASIDE.

TO MAKE THE BÉCHAMEL SAUCE: MELT BUTTER, ADD FLOUR AND SEASONINGS AND STIR FOR A FEW MINUTES. ADD MILK, STIRRING CONSTANTLY. COOK SLOWLY UNTIL THICKENED.

TO MAKE LASAGNE: COOK PASTA ACCORDING TO PACKAGE DIRECTIONS. DRAIN, PLUNGE INTO COLD WATER AND SET ASIDE. LADLE $\frac{1}{3}$ OF BÉCHAMEL SAUCE INTO BOTTOM OF 9" X 13" PAN. THEN LAYER PASTA, TOMATO SAUCE, BOCCONCINI AND PESTO. REPEAT LAYERS AND FINISH WITH GRATED PARMESAN. BAKE AT 350°F FOR 40 MINUTES. GOOD AS A SIDE DISH WITH GRILLED CHICKEN. SERVES 12.

I KNOW A MAN WHO IS SO RICH, HE DOESN'T EVEN KNOW HIS SON IS IN COLLEGE.

PASTA PIE

A DAY-AHEAD MAKE-AHEAD. GOOD FAMILY FARE.

SAUCE

1 LB. BULK ITALIAN SAUSAGE OR LEAN GROUND BEEF	500 g
1/2 CUP CHOPPED ONION	125 mL
1/4 CUP CHOPPED GREEN PEPPER	60 mL
14 OZ. CAN TOMATOES, CHOPPED	398 mL
5 1/2 OZ. CAN TOMATO PASTE	156 mL
1/2 CUP WATER	125 mL
1 TSP. SUGAR	5 mL
1 TSP. DRIED OREGANO	5 mL
1 TSP. DRIED BASIL	5 mL
1/2 TSP. GARLIC POWDER	2 mL

SHELL

6 OZ. PASTA, SPAGHETTI OR LINGUINE (TO MAKE 4 CUPS, COOKED)	170 g
2 TBSP. MARGARINE	30 mL
1/2 CUP GRATED PARMESAN CHEESE	125 mL
2 EGGS, WELL-BEATEN	
1 CUP RICOTTA CHEESE	250 mL
1 CUP GRATED MOZZARELLA CHEESE	250 mL

TO MAKE SAUCE: SAUTÉ MEAT, ONIONS AND GREEN PEPPERS IN LARGE SKILLET UNTIL MEAT IS BROWNED. DRAIN OFF FAT. ADD REMAINING SAUCE INGREDIENTS AND SIMMER FOR 30 MINUTES.

TO MAKE SHELL: COOK PASTA ACCORDING TO PACKAGE DIRECTIONS, DRAIN. STIR IN

PASTA PIE

THIS RECIPE CONTINUED FROM PAGE 148.

MARGARINE AND PARMESAN. ADD EGGS AND STIR WELL. PRESS PASTA INTO BOTTOM AND SIDES OF A 10" PIE PLATE TO FORM A SHELL.

SPREAD RICOTTA OVER PASTA SHELL AND TOP WITH MEAT SAUCE. COVER WITH FOIL AND REFRIGERATE UNTIL WELL-CHILLED OR UP TO 24 HOURS. BAKE, COVERED, AT 350°F FOR ONE HOUR. UNCOVER, TOP WITH MOZZARELLA AND BAKE UNTIL CHEESE MELTS. SERVES 6.

PASTA WITH PEPPERS

AFTER FIVE AND STILL ALIVE!

4 PEPPERS, USE MIXTURE OF RED, GREEN & YELLOW	
1/3 CUP OLIVE OIL	75 mL
3 GARLIC CLOVES, MINCED	
1/2 LB. SPAGHETTINI	250 g
2 CUPS GRATED ASIAGO OR FRESHLY GRATED PARMESAN CHEESE	500 mL

CUT PEPPERS INTO STRIPS. SAUTÉ IN OIL WITH GARLIC. COOK PASTA ACCORDING TO PACKAGE DIRECTIONS. DRAIN. POUR PEPPER-OIL MIXTURE OVER HOT PASTA AND TOSS WITH GRATED CHEESE. SERVES 4 AS A SIDE DISH.

CREAMY MUSHROOM PASTA

THE SPINACH ADDS FLAVOR AND COLOR TO THIS
DELICIOUS PASTA DISH.

1 TBSP. BUTTER	15 mL
1 TBSP. OIL	15 mL
4 CUPS SLICED MUSHROOMS	1 L
2 SHALLOTS, FINELY CHOPPED	
1 TBSP. MADEIRA OR DRY SHERRY	15 mL
12 OZ. FETTUCCINE	340 g
1½ CUPS WHIPPING CREAM	375 mL
3 CUPS FRESH SPINACH LEAVES,	750 mL
CUT IN STRIPS	
SALT & FRESHLY GROUND PEPPER	
FRESHLY GRATED PARMESAN CHEESE	

MELT BUTTER AND OIL IN SKILLET. ADD
MUSHROOMS AND COOK OVER MEDIUM HEAT UNTIL
SOFT. ADD SHALLOTS AND SAUTÉ ONE MINUTE.
ADD SHERRY. COOK, UNCOVERED, 8-10 MINUTES OR
UNTIL MOST OF THE LIQUID HAS EVAPORATED.
STIR OCCASIONALLY. COOK PASTA ACCORDING TO
PACKAGE DIRECTIONS. DRAIN WELL - DON'T
RINSE! ADD CREAM AND SPINACH TO MUSHROOMS
AND BOIL MIXTURE GENTLY FOR ABOUT 5
MINUTES UNTIL SAUCE HAS THICKENED SLIGHTLY.
ADD SALT AND PEPPER. TOSS HOT SAUCE WITH
PASTA AND SERVE IMMEDIATELY WITH LOTS OF
PARMESAN CHEESE. SERVES 4.

I HAVE LEARNED TO SPELL HORS D'OEUVRE,
WHICH GETS ON MANY PEOPLE'S NERVES.

ROTINI AND SHRIMP IN CURRY GARLIC CREAM

¼ CUP MINCED FRESH PARSLEY	60 mL
2 GARLIC CLOVES, MINCED	
1 TBSP. MARGARINE OR BUTTER	15 mL
⅓ CUP WHITE WINE	75 mL
1-2 TSP. CURRY POWDER	5-10 mL
½ LB. SHRIMP, PEELED & DEVEINED	250 g
1½ CUPS HALF & HALF CREAM	375 mL
½ CUP GRATED PARMESAN CHEESE	125 mL
¼ TSP. NUTMEG	1 mL
SALT & FRESHLY GROUND PEPPER TO TASTE	
1 LB. ROTINI	500 g

COOK PARSLEY AND GARLIC IN BUTTER OVER MEDIUM HEAT. ADD WINE AND REDUCE HEAT, STIRRING FOR 2-3 MINUTES. ADD CURRY POWDER AND SHRIMP, STIRRING UNTIL SHRIMP ARE PINK. BLEND IN CREAM AND SIMMER FOR 2 MINUTES. REMOVE FROM HEAT AND ADD PARMESAN CHEESE, NUTMEG, SALT AND PEPPER. KEEP WARM. COOK PASTA ACCORDING TO PACKAGE DIRECTIONS. DRAIN WELL AND POUR SAUCE OVER PASTA. TOSS GENTLY AND SERVE HOT WITH A GREEN SALAD. SERVES 4.

A FOOL AND HIS MONEY NEVER APPEAR WHEN YOU NEED A LOAN.

CHICKEN WITH SPAGHETTINI

A NIFTY NOODLE DISH WITH A WONDERFUL TARRAGON FLAVOR.

2 CHICKEN BREASTS, SKINNED AND BONED	
1/4 CUP BUTTER OR MARGARINE	60 mL
3 GARLIC CLOVES, MINCED	
1 ONION, FINELY CHOPPED	
3 MEDIUM TOMATOES, CHOPPED	
1 TBSP. DRIED TARRAGON OR BASIL	15 mL
3/4 LB. SPAGHETTINI OR LINGUINE	375 g
3 TBSP. DRY WHITE WINE OR VERMOUTH	45 mL
1/4 CUP CHICKEN STOCK	60 mL
1 CUP WHIPPING CREAM	250 mL
1/4 TSP. EACH SALT & PEPPER	1 mL
1/2 CUP CHOPPED FRESH PARSLEY	125 mL
FRESHLY GRATED PARMESAN CHEESE	

CUT CHICKEN IN CUBES AND SAUTÉ IN BUTTER STIRRING UNTIL DONE. TRANSFER TO A PLATE. ADD GARLIC AND ONION TO SKILLET. SAUTÉ UNTIL SOFTENED. ADD TOMATOES AND TARRAGON AND COOK 3 MINUTES. COOK SPAGHETTINI ACCORDING TO PACKAGE DIRECTIONS. DRAIN. MEANWHILE, POUR WINE AND STOCK INTO SKILLET AND COOK UNTIL REDUCED BY TWO-THIRDS. STIR IN CREAM, SALT AND PEPPER AND COOK UNTIL SLIGHTLY THICKENED. ADD COOKED CHICKEN AND ACCUMULATED JUICES AND SIMMER UNTIL HEATED THROUGH. STIR IN 1/3 CUP PARSLEY AND TOSS WITH HOT PASTA IN LARGE SERVING BOWL. TOP WITH REMAINING PARSLEY. PASS THE PARMESAN. SERVES 4.

QUICK PEROGY CASSEROLE

16 OZ. PKG. FROZEN PEROGIES	500 g
3 TBSP. OIL	45 mL
2 LARGE ONIONS, THINLY SLICED	
1 CUP SLICED MUSHROOMS	250 mL
14 OZ. CAN TOMATOES, DICED	398 mL
1 TBSP. CHOPPED PARSLEY	15 mL
3/4 TSP. SALT	3 mL
1/4 TSP. PEPPER	1 mL
1 CUP WATER	250 mL

PREPARE PEROGIES AS PACKAGE DIRECTS FOR BOILED PEROGIES. DRAIN. IN A LARGE SKILLET, HEAT OIL, ADD ONIONS AND MUSHROOMS. COOK UNTIL SOFT AND GOLDEN. ADD REMAINING INGREDIENTS AND BRING TO A BOIL. COOK FOR 5 MINUTES.

PREHEAT OVEN TO 350°F. IN A SHALLOW 2-QUART CASSEROLE, ARRANGE PEROGIES AND COVER WITH ONION MIXTURE. BAKE, COVERED, FOR 30 MINUTES. SERVES 4.

WHY IS THE WRONG NUMBER ON THE TELEPHONE NEVER BUSY?

FETTUCCINE FLORENTINE

1 LB. BACON	500 g
1 LB. FETTUCCINE	500 g
½ CUP BUTTER OR MARGARINE	125 mL
3-4 CUPS CHOPPED FRESH SPINACH	750 mL–1 L
1½ CUPS CREAM	375 mL
1 EGG, LIGHTLY BEATEN	
1 CUP FRESHLY GRATED PARMESAN CHEESE	250 mL
SALT & FRESHLY GROUND BLACK PEPPER TO TASTE	

COOK BACON UNTIL CRISP AND THEN CRUMBLE. COOK THE PASTA ACCORDING TO PACKAGE DIRECTIONS. MELT THE BUTTER IN A LARGE SAUCEPAN. ADD THE SPINACH AND BACON AND SAUTÉ UNTIL HEATED THROUGH. ADD THE FETTUCCINE AND TOSS. COMBINE THE CREAM AND EGG IN A SMALL BOWL, THEN POUR OVER THE PASTA. ADD THE CHEESE AND MIX WELL. SEASON WITH SALT AND PEPPER. HEAT THOROUGHLY BUT DO NOT COOK. SERVE IMMEDIATELY. VERY RICH. SERVES 4-6.

IF HOSPITALS ARE PLACES TO GET WELL, WHY DO THEY SERVE THAT FOOD?

GRANDMA HUDSON'S GRANOLA COOKIES

JOHNNY'S FAVORITE.

1 CUP BUTTER OR MARGARINE	250 mL
3/4 CUP BROWN SUGAR	175 mL
3/4 CUP WHITE SUGAR	175 mL
1 TSP. VANILLA	5 mL
2 EGGS	
1 CUP WHOLE-WHEAT FLOUR	250 mL
1 CUP WHITE FLOUR	250 mL
1 TSP. BAKING POWDER	5 mL
1 TSP. BAKING SODA	5 mL
1 CUP COCONUT	250 mL
1 CUP OATMEAL	250 mL
1 CUP RICE KRISPIES	250 mL
1 CUP RAISINS	250 mL
1 CUP CHOCOLATE CHIPS	250 mL
3/4 CUP SUNFLOWER SEEDS	175 mL
1/2 CUP SESAME SEEDS	125 mL
1/3 CUP FLAX SEEDS (OPTIONAL)	75 mL
1/3 CUP WHEAT GERM	75 mL

PREHEAT OVEN TO 350°F. IN A LARGE MIXING BOWL, BEAT TOGETHER BUTTER, SUGARS, VANILLA AND EGGS. ADD FLOURS, BAKING POWDER AND BAKING SODA. CONTINUE BEATING UNTIL WELL-BLENDED. ADD REMAINING INGREDIENTS. MIX WELL. ROLL INTO BALLS AND PLACE ON GREASED COOKIE SHEET AND FLATTEN WITH A FORK. BAKE AT 350°F FOR 10 MINUTES. MAKES DOZENS.

NEVER PLAY LEAPFROG WITH A UNICORN.

CHOCOLATE-CHOCOLATE CHIP COOKIES

YUMMY - TASTES LIKE A BROWNIE!

1¾ CUPS FLOUR	425 mL
¾ TSP. BAKING SODA	3 mL
1 CUP BUTTER OR MARGARINE	250 mL
1 TSP. VANILLA	5 mL
1 CUP SUGAR	250 mL
½ CUP PACKED BROWN SUGAR	125 mL
1 EGG	
⅓ CUP COCOA	75 mL
2 TBSP. MILK	30 mL
1 CUP CHOPPED PECANS OR WALNUTS	250 mL
¾ CUP SEMI-SWEET CHOCOLATE CHIPS	175 mL

PREHEAT OVEN TO 350°F. IN A LARGE MIXING BOWL, STIR TOGETHER FLOUR AND BAKING SODA. SET ASIDE. CREAM BUTTER, ADD VANILLA AND SUGARS. BEAT UNTIL FLUFFY. BEAT IN EGG, THEN COCOA, THEN MILK. MIX IN FLOUR UNTIL JUST BLENDED. STIR IN NUTS AND CHOCOLATE CHIPS. DROP BY SPOONFULS ON GREASED COOKIE SHEETS AND BAKE FOR 12 MINUTES. COOL SLIGHTLY BEFORE REMOVING FROM COOKIE SHEET. MAKES 3 DOZEN.

A PEDESTRIAN IS A MAN WHOSE CHILD IS HOME FROM COLLEGE.

MACADAMIA CHOCOLATE COOKIES

BAKE THESE FOR SOMEONE SPECIAL!

2 - 1 OZ. SQUARES UNSWEETENED CHOCOLATE	55 g
½ CUP BUTTER, SOFTENED	125 mL
1 CUP PACKED BROWN SUGAR	250 mL
1 EGG	
1 TSP. VANILLA	5 mL
1¼ CUPS FLOUR	300 mL
½ TSP. BAKING SODA	2 mL
1 CUP WHITE CHOCOLATE CHIPS	250 mL
1 CUP MACADAMIA NUTS, COARSELY CHOPPED	250 mL

PREHEAT OVEN TO 350°F. MELT CHOCOLATE SQUARES AND COOL TO ROOM TEMPERATURE. CREAM BUTTER, BROWN SUGAR AND MELTED CHOCOLATE. ADD EGG AND VANILLA AND BEAT UNTIL BLENDED. BLEND IN FLOUR, BAKING SODA, CHOCOLATE CHIPS AND NUTS. DROP BY SPOONFULS ONTO A GREASED COOKIE SHEET. BAKE 8-10 MINUTES. MAKES 3 DOZEN.

MIDDLE AGE IS ABOUT 10 YEARS OLDER THAN YOU ARE.

FRESH APPLE COOKIES

TEACHER'S CHOICE.

2 CUPS FLOUR	500 mL
1 TSP. BAKING SODA	5 mL
½ CUP BUTTER, SOFTENED	125 mL
1⅓ CUPS PACKED BROWN SUGAR	325 mL
½ TSP. SALT	2 mL
1 TSP. CINNAMON	5 mL
1 TSP. GROUND CLOVES	5 mL
½ TSP. NUTMEG	2 mL
1 EGG, BEATEN	
¼ CUP APPLE JUICE OR MILK	60 mL
1 CUP CHOPPED APPLES	250 mL
½-1 CUP CHOPPED NUTS	125-250 mL
1 CUP RAISINS	250 mL

VANILLA GLAZE

1 CUP ICING SUGAR	250 mL
1 TBSP. BUTTER, SOFTENED	15 mL
¼ TSP. VANILLA	1 mL
¼ TSP. SALT	1 mL
1½ TBSP. MILK	22 mL

TO MAKE COOKIES: PREHEAT OVEN TO 375°F. COMBINE FLOUR AND BAKING SODA IN MEDIUM BOWL. IN A LARGE BOWL, CREAM TOGETHER BUTTER, BROWN SUGAR, SALT, CINNAMON, CLOVES, NUTMEG AND EGG. ADD HALF THE FLOUR TO THE BUTTER MIXTURE AND BLEND WELL. MIX IN JUICE OR MILK. ADD THE APPLES, NUTS AND RAISINS TO THE REMAINING FLOUR. ADD THIS APPLE MIXTURE TO THE BUTTER MIXTURE.

FRESH APPLE COOKIES

THIS RECIPE CONTINUED FROM PAGE 158.

DROP BY SPOONFULS ON GREASED COOKIE SHEETS AND BAKE FOR 10 MINUTES OR UNTIL COOKIES ARE FIRM.

TO MAKE GLAZE: BLEND ALL INGREDIENTS TOGETHER UNTIL SMOOTH. WHILE COOKIES ARE HOT, SPREAD WITH VANILLA GLAZE. MAKES 3 DOZEN

ORANGE CHOCOLATE CHIP COOKIES

1 CUP MARGARINE	250 mL
1 CUP BROWN SUGAR	250 mL
1 CUP WHITE SUGAR	250 mL
2 EGGS	
1 TSP. VANILLA	5 mL
3 CUPS OATMEAL	750 mL
2 CUPS FLOUR	500 mL
1 TSP. SALT	5 mL
1 TSP. BAKING SODA	5 mL
GRATED RIND OF 1 ORANGE	
1 ORANGE, PEELED & CHOPPED	
2 CUPS CHOCOLATE CHIPS	500 mL

PREHEAT OVEN TO 350°F. IN A LARGE MIXING BOWL, CREAM MARGARINE AND SUGARS TOGETHER. ADD EGGS AND VANILLA. BEAT UNTIL SMOOTH. ADD DRY INGREDIENTS, RIND AND ORANGE TO CREAMED MIXTURE, MIXING WELL. STIR IN CHOCOLATE CHIPS. DROP BY SPOONFULS ONTO A GREASED COOKIE SHEET AND FLATTEN WITH A FORK. BAKE FOR 10-12 MINUTES, OR UNTIL LIGHTLY BROWNED. MAKES 4 DOZEN.

NANNY'S REAL SCOTTISH SHORTBREAD

HOOT MON, I WANT TO MEET NANNY!

1 LB. BUTTER	454 g
1 CUP BERRY SUGAR	250 mL
3 CUPS FLOUR	750 mL
1 CUP RICE FLOUR	250 mL
2 TSP. BAKING POWDER	10 mL
GLACÉ CHERRIES, HALVED	

PREHEAT OVEN TO 300°F. USING ELECTRIC MIXER, CREAM BUTTER AND SUGAR UNTIL SMOOTH. GRADUALLY ADD FLOURS AND BAKING POWDER AND CONTINUE BEATING FOR SEVERAL MINUTES UNTIL WELL-MIXED. KNEAD DOUGH UNTIL SHINY. ROLL DOUGH FAIRLY THICK, 1/4", AND CUT WITH COOKIE CUTTER. DECORATE WITH HALVED GLACÉ CHERRIES. BAKE FOR 15-20 MINUTES OR UNTIL EDGES ARE LIGHTLY GOLDEN. MAKES A TIN FULL.

JUST WHEN YOU GET TO THE POINT WHERE MENU PRICES DON'T MATTER, CALORIES DO!

BISCOTTI

AN AFTER-DINNER TREAT SERVED WITH A SWEET DESSERT WINE OR CAPPUCCINO. MAMMA SAYS, "DUNK BISCOTTI!"

½ CUP BUTTER	125 mL
¾ CUP SUGAR	175 mL
3 EGGS	
½ TSP. VANILLA	2 mL
3 CUPS FLOUR	750 mL
1 TBSP. BAKING POWDER	15 mL
½ TSP. SALT	2 mL
1 TBSP. ANISEED	15 mL
2 TBSP. GRATED LEMON RIND	30 mL
2 TBSP. GRATED ORANGE RIND	30 mL
1 CUP CHOPPED BLANCHED ALMONDS	250 mL

PREHEAT OVEN TO 350°F. CREAM BUTTER AND SUGAR TOGETHER UNTIL LIGHT AND FLUFFY. ADD EGGS ONE AT A TIME, BEATING WELL. ADD VANILLA. COMBINE FLOUR, BAKING POWDER AND SALT AND STIR INTO THE BATTER. ADD REMAINING INGREDIENTS AND BLEND WELL. DIVIDE DOUGH INTO 3 PARTS AND SHAPE INTO ROLLS 1½" IN DIAMETER. PLACE EACH ROLL ON A SEPARATE COOKIE SHEET, FLATTEN THE TOP SLIGHTLY AND BAKE 15 MINUTES. REMOVE FROM THE OVEN AND CUT EACH ROLL INTO ¾" SLICES. PLACE CUT SIDE DOWN ON SHEET. RETURN TO OVEN AND BAKE 15 MINUTES LONGER. COOL ON A RACK. MAKES ABOUT 4 DOZEN.

SNICKERDOODLES

A 19TH CENTURY NONSENSE WORD MEANING "A QUICK-TO-MAKE CONFECTION!"

DOUGH

2⅔ CUPS FLOUR	650 mL
1 CUP MARGARINE OR BUTTER	250 mL
2 TSP. CREAM OF TARTAR	10 mL
1 TSP. BAKING SODA	5 mL
½ TSP. SALT	2 mL
½ TSP. VANILLA	2 mL
2 EGGS	
1¼ CUPS SUGAR	300 mL

COATING

2 TSP. CINNAMON	10 mL
2 TBSP. SUGAR	30 mL

IN A LARGE BOWL, MIX THE DOUGH INGREDIENTS AT LOW SPEED, BEATING UNTIL WELL-BLENDED. SHAPE DOUGH INTO A BALL AND WRAP IN PLASTIC WRAP. REFRIGERATE FOR 2 HOURS OR CAN BE LEFT IN THE REFRIGERATOR FOR ONE WEEK. PREHEAT OVEN TO 400°F. IN A SMALL BOWL, MIX CINNAMON AND SUGAR. ROLL DOUGH INTO 1½" BALLS, THEN ROLL IN CINNAMON-SUGAR MIXTURE TO COAT LIGHTLY. PLACE BALLS 2" APART ON UNGREASED COOKIE SHEET. IF YOU LIKE, PRESS PARALLEL LINES IN EACH COOKIE WITH THE DULL EDGE OF A KNIFE. BAKE 10-12 MINUTES UNTIL LIGHTLY BROWNED.
MAKES 2½-3 DOZEN COOKIES.

CHOCOLATE TRUFFLE COOKIES

GIFTABLE! PLACE IN SMALL PAPER MUFFIN CUPS AND PRESENT IN COOKIE TINS.

1 CUP BUTTER, SOFTENED	250 mL
½ CUP ICING SUGAR	125 mL
1½ TSP. VANILLA	7 mL
1 OZ. SQUARE UNSWEETENED CHOCOLATE, MELTED	30 g
2¼ CUPS FLOUR	530 mL
¼ TSP. SALT	1 mL
1 CUP SEMI-SWEET CHOCOLATE CHIPS	250 mL

COATING

¼ CUP ICING SUGAR	60 mL
2 TBSP. COCOA	30 mL

PREHEAT OVEN TO 375°F. LIGHTLY GREASE COOKIE SHEETS. IN A LARGE BOWL, CREAM BUTTER AND ½ CUP ICING SUGAR. BLEND IN VANILLA AND MELTED CHOCOLATE. AT LOW SPEED, BLEND IN FLOUR AND SALT. STIR IN CHOCOLATE CHIPS. SHAPE INTO ONE-INCH BALLS AND PLACE ON COOKIE SHEET. BAKE FOR 10 MINUTES AND COOL. IN A SMALL BOWL, COMBINE ICING SUGAR AND COCOA, ROLL COOLED COOKIES IN COCOA MIXTURE. STORE IN AN AIRTIGHT CONTAINER. MAKES 4 DOZEN.

ONE KIND OF MOTORIST WHO NEVER RUNS OUT OF GAS IS A BACK-SEAT DRIVER.

MACAROONS

DIRECT FROM THE GOLDEN GIRLS.

3 CUPS FLAKED COCONUT	750 mL
1/2 CUP FLOUR	125 mL
1/4 TSP. SALT	1 mL
10 OZ. CAN SWEETENED CONDENSED MILK	284 mL
1 TSP. VANILLA	5 mL
1 CUP FLAKED ALMONDS, TOASTED	250 mL
RED & GREEN CHERRIES, CHOPPED	

PREHEAT OVEN TO 325°F. COMBINE ALL INGREDIENTS EXCEPT CHERRIES. DROP BATTER BY TEASPOONFULS ONTO GREASED COOKIE SHEET. TOP EACH MACAROON WITH A PIECE OF CHERRY. BAKE 10-15 MINUTES. MAKES APPROXIMATELY 4 DOZEN.

PEPPERMINT BRITTLE

2 LBS. WHITE CHOCOLATE (BULK IS BEST)	1 kg
1-1½ CUPS CRUSHED CANDY CANES	250-375 mL

LINE A 10" X 15" EDGED COOKIE SHEET WITH HEAVY-DUTY FOIL. BREAK UP CHOCOLATE AND MELT OVER LOW HEAT. BE VERY CAREFUL NOT TO BURN. ADD CRUSHED CANDY TO CHOCOLATE AND POUR INTO PAN AND CHILL UNTIL SET (ABOUT ONE HOUR). BREAK INTO PIECES BY SLAMMING PAN ON COUNTER.

GRAND MARNIER CHOCOLATE TRUFFLES

DELECTABLE! GIFTABLE! AND VERY EASY TO MAKE!

2 - 4 OZ. PLAIN MILK CHOCOLATE BARS (SWISS, BELGIAN OR DUTCH)	227 g
2-3 TBSP. WHIPPING CREAM	30-45 mL
2 TBSP. GRAND MARNIER	30 mL
1 EGG, SLIGHTLY BEATEN	
3/4 TSP. GRATED ORANGE RIND	3 mL
2 TBSP. BUTTER	30 mL

COATINGS

COCOA, CHOCOLATE SPRINKLES OR TOASTED CHOPPED NUTS.

MELT CHOCOLATE OVER LOW HEAT IN DOUBLE BOILER. WARM WHIPPING CREAM. STIR INTO CHOCOLATE ALONG WITH LIQUEUR. WHISK IN EGG, ORANGE RIND AND BUTTER UNTIL MIXTURE IS SMOOTH. REFRIGERATE ABOUT 2 HOURS, UNTIL FIRM. USING A TEASPOON, SCOOP OUT CHOCOLATE. ROLL INTO BALLS. ROLL IN COATING OF CHOICE. REFRIGERATE UNTIL SERVING. THESE MAY ALSO BE FROZEN. OTHER LIQUEURS OR COGNAC MAY BE SUBSTITUTED. MAKES ABOUT 25-30 TRUFFLES.

SEEING IS DECEIVING - IT'S EATING THAT'S BELIEVING.

MY LATEST FAVORITE CAKE

THIS IS GOOD OL' FASHIONED COOKIN'!

CAKE

1 CUP BOILING WATER	250 mL
½ CUP BUTTER	125 mL
2 CUPS BROWN SUGAR	500 mL
1 CUP OATMEAL (NOT INSTANT)	250 mL
2 EGGS, BEATEN	
1 CUP FLOUR	250 mL
1 TSP. CINNAMON	5 mL
¾ TSP. ALLSPICE	3 mL
1 TSP. BAKING SODA	5 mL
½ CUP CUT UP PITTED DATES	125 mL
½ CUP CHOPPED NUTS	125 mL

ICING

1 CUP BROWN SUGAR	250 mL
5 TBSP. BUTTER	75 mL
¼ CUP MILK	60 mL
ICING SUGAR TO THICKEN	

PREHEAT OVEN TO 350°F. IN A LARGE BOWL, POUR BOILING WATER OVER BUTTER, BROWN SUGAR AND OATMEAL AND LET STAND 20 MINUTES. ADD REMAINING INGREDIENTS AND MIX WELL. BAKE IN A GREASED 8" X 8" PAN FOR 35-40 MINUTES, OR UNTIL AN INSERTED TOOTHPICK COMES OUT CLEAN.

FOR ICING: BOIL AND STIR BROWN SUGAR, BUTTER AND MILK FOR 5 MINUTES. THICKEN WITH ICING SUGAR. ICE CAKE WHILE WARM.

SOUR CREAM APPLE CAKE

MOIST AND DELICIOUS.

2 CUPS FLOUR	500 mL
2 CUPS BROWN SUGAR	500 mL
½ CUP BUTTER OR MARGARINE, SOFTENED	125 mL
1 CUP CHOPPED NUTS	250 mL
1½ TSP. CINNAMON	7 mL
1 TSP. BAKING SODA	5 mL
½ TSP. SALT	2 mL
1 CUP SOUR CREAM	250 mL
1 TSP. VANILLA	5 mL
1 EGG	
2 CUPS FINELY CHOPPED, PEELED APPLES	500 mL

WHIPPED CREAM OR ICE CREAM TO SERVE

PREHEAT OVEN TO 350°F. IN A LARGE BOWL, COMBINE FLOUR, BROWN SUGAR AND BUTTER. MIX ON LOW SPEED UNTIL CRUMBLY. STIR IN NUTS. NOW, REMOVE ONLY 2¾ CUPS OF THE CRUMB MIXTURE FROM THE BOWL. PRESS THIS INTO AN UNGREASED 9" X 13" PAN. TO THE REST OF THE CRUMB MIXTURE, ADD CINNAMON, BAKING SODA, SALT, SOUR CREAM, VANILLA AND EGG. BLEND WELL. STIR IN APPLES. SPOON EVENLY OVER CRUST. BAKE 30 MINUTES, OR UNTIL TOOTHPICK COMES OUT CLEAN. CUT INTO SERVING-SIZED SQUARES AND SERVE WARM WITH WHIPPED CREAM OR ICE CREAM.

PLUM RUM CAKE

THIS WILL APPEAL TO THE BIGGEST "BABY" IN YOUR FAMILY

CAKE

2 CUPS FLOUR	500 mL
2 CUPS SUGAR	500 mL
1 TSP. CINNAMON	5 mL
1 TSP. CLOVES	5 mL
1 TSP. BAKING POWDER	5 mL
1 TSP. SALT	5 mL
3 EGGS	
1 CUP OIL	250 mL
2 - 4½ OZ. JARS PLUM BABY FOOD	2 - 128 mL
3 TBSP. DARK RUM	45 mL

GLAZE

1 CUP ICING SUGAR	250 mL
2-3 TBSP. LEMON JUICE	30-45 mL
2 TSP. DARK RUM	10 mL

PREHEAT OVEN TO 350°F. GREASE AND FLOUR A 10" BUNDT PAN. SIFT TOGETHER DRY INGREDIENTS. ADD EGGS AND OIL AND BEAT AT SLOW SPEED. ADD BABY FOOD AND RUM. MIX WELL. BAKE FOR 40 MINUTES. COOL 10 MINUTES AND REMOVE FROM PAN. MIX GLAZE AND POUR OVER CAKE WHILE STILL WARM.

DOES LIFE BEGIN AT BIRTH, OR AFTER YOU'VE HAD YOUR FIRST MARTINI?

CHERRY-FILLED ANGEL CAKE

A BLAST FROM THE PAST!

10 OZ. PKG. FROZEN PITTED SWEET DARK CHERRIES	285 g
1/3 CUP SUGAR	75 mL
1 TBSP. CORNSTARCH	15 mL
10" ANGEL FOOD CAKE	25 cm
3 CUPS WHIPPING CREAM	750 mL
2 TBSP. ALMOND OR CHERRY LIQUEUR OR 1 TSP. (5 mL) VANILLA OR ALMOND FLAVORING	30 mL

THAW CHERRIES ENOUGH TO SEPARATE. TOSS WITH SUGAR AND CORNSTARCH. COOK OVER MEDIUM HEAT, STIRRING UNTIL MIXTURE BOILS AND IS THICKENED AND CLEAR. LET COOL. WITH A SERRATED KNIFE, CUT 3/4" SLICE FROM TOP OF CAKE. HOLLOW OUT CAKE, LEAVING SIDES 3/4" THICK. TEAR REMOVED CAKE PIECES INTO BITE-SIZED CHUNKS AND PLACE IN BOWL. WHIP ONE CUP OF THE CREAM WITH ONE TBSP. OF THE LIQUEUR. FOLD INTO CAKE PIECES ALONG WITH COOLED CHERRY MIXTURE. SPOON INTO HOLLOWED-OUT CAKE, REPLACE TOP SLICE. (THIS MUCH CAN BE DONE THE DAY BEFORE.) COVER AND REFRIGERATE.

BEFORE SERVING, WHIP REMAINING CREAM WITH LIQUEUR. FROST CAKE. COVER AND REFRIGERATE UNTIL READY TO SERVE.

FRESH APPLE CAKE

EVE COULD HAVE PUT HER APPLES TO BETTER USE!

CAKE

3 TART APPLES, PEELED & CHOPPED	
3 TBSP. SUGAR	45 mL
2 TSP. CINNAMON	10 mL
2 CUPS SUGAR	500 mL
1 CUP VEGETABLE OIL	250 mL
4 EGGS	
¼ CUP ORANGE JUICE	60 mL
1 TSP. ORANGE RIND	5 mL
2 TSP. VANILLA	10 mL
3 CUPS FLOUR	750 mL
1 TBSP. BAKING POWDER	15 mL
½ TSP. SALT	2 mL

GLAZE

1 CUP ORANGE JUICE	250 mL
2 TBSP. LEMON JUICE	30 mL
1 CUP SUGAR	250 mL
2 TBSP. RUM	30 mL

COMBINE APPLES WITH SUGAR AND CINNAMON. SET ASIDE. IN A LARGE BOWL, BEAT SUGAR AND OIL. ADD EGGS, ONE AT A TIME, BEATING AFTER EACH ADDITION. ADD ORANGE JUICE, RIND AND VANILLA. COMBINE FLOUR, BAKING POWDER AND SALT. BEAT INTO CREAMED MIXTURE UNTIL SMOOTH. GREASE A 10" BUNDT OR TUBE PAN. POUR ⅓ BATTER INTO PAN, THEN ½ OF THE

FRESH APPLE CAKE

THIS RECIPE CONTINUED FROM PAGE 170.

APPLES. REPEAT ⅓ BATTER, ½ APPLES AND FINAL ⅓ BATTER. BAKE AT 350°F FOR 60-70 MINUTES, OR UNTIL INSERTED TOOTHPICK COMES OUT CLEAN. COOL SLIGHTLY BEFORE GLAZING.

FOR THE GLAZE: COMBINE ALL INGREDIENTS IN POT AND BRING TO A BOIL. DRIZZLE OVER WARM CAKE BEFORE REMOVING FROM PAN.

CHEDDAR APPLE TART

APPLE PIE WITHOUT CHEESE IS LIKE A KISS WITHOUT A SQUEEZE!

PASTRY

2 CUPS FLOUR	500 mL
½ TSP. SALT	2 mL
1½ CUPS GRATED OLD CHEDDAR CHEESE	375 mL
½ CUP BUTTER	125 mL
¼ CUP COLD WATER	60 mL

FILLING

5 CUPS PEELED & CHOPPED APPLES	1.25 L
½ CUP SUGAR	125 mL
2 TBSP. MINUTE TAPIOCA	30 mL
2 TBSP. FLOUR	30 mL
1 TBSP. LEMON JUICE	15 mL
2 TBSP. MELTED BUTTER	30 mL
1 TSP. CINNAMON	5 mL

CONTINUED ON PAGE 172.

CHEDDAR APPLE TART

THIS RECIPE CONTINUED FROM PAGE 171.

TO MAKE PASTRY: IN A LARGE BOWL, STIR TOGETHER FLOUR, SALT AND CHEESE. CUT BUTTER INTO THIS MIXTURE UNTIL CONSISTENCY RESEMBLES SMALL PEAS. ADD WATER GRADUALLY AND BLEND MIXTURE TO FORM A BALL. ROLL PASTRY ON A FLOURED SURFACE UNTIL ¼" THICK. LINE A 9" PIE PLATE OR CUT INTO 16 TART SHELLS. USE REMAINING DOUGH FOR LATTICE OR "CUT OUTS" ON TOP OF FILLING.

TO MAKE FILLING: IN A LARGE MIXING BOWL, COMBINE ALL FILLING INGREDIENTS. FILL PIE OR TARTS. TOP WITH REMAINING PASTRY IF DESIRED. BAKE AT 350°F. 20 MINUTES FOR TARTS OR 45 MINUTES FOR PIE, UNTIL CRUST IS GOLDEN AND APPLE MIXTURE IS BUBBLY.

IF ALL THE MORALISTS IN THE WORLD WERE LAID END TO END - IT WOULD BE A GOOD THING.

PICTURED ON OVERLEAF

FRESH BERRY TART - PAGE 202

ACES - PAGE 186

RASPBERRY-WALNUT LINZER BARS

1½ CUPS BUTTER, SOFTENED	375 mL
1 CUP ICING SUGAR	250 mL
1 EGG	
¼ TSP. SALT	1 mL
½ TSP. CINNAMON	2 mL
2¾ CUPS FLOUR	675 mL
1½ CUPS FINELY CHOPPED WALNUTS OR PECANS	375 mL
2 CUPS RASPBERRY JAM	500 mL
1 TBSP. LEMON JUICE	15 mL
ICING SUGAR TO SPRINKLE	

CREAM BUTTER, SUGAR, EGG, SALT AND CINNAMON UNTIL FLUFFY. FOLD IN FLOUR AND NUTS. CHILL DOUGH ONE HOUR OR UNTIL STIFF ENOUGH TO HANDLE. SET ASIDE ⅓ OF DOUGH. PAT REMAINING ⅔ OF DOUGH INTO A 10" X 15" EDGED COOKIE SHEET. STIR TOGETHER JAM AND LEMON JUICE. SPREAD EVENLY OVER PASTRY. ON A FLOURED SURFACE, PAT OR ROLL OUT REMAINING DOUGH INTO A RECTANGLE. CUT INTO STRIPS ¼" WIDE. PLACE STRIPS ON TOP OF JAM IN A LATTICE PATTERN. DON'T WORRY IF DOUGH BREAKS WHEN YOU ARE MAKING THE PATTERN - JUST PINCH IT TOGETHER. IT'LL BAKE INTO ONE PIECE. BAKE AT 375°F FOR 35-40 MINUTES, UNTIL PASTRY IS LIGHTLY BROWNED. COOL. SPRINKLE WITH ICING SUGAR. CUT INTO BARS.

A YAWN MAY BE BAD MANNERS, BUT IT'S AN HONEST OPINION.

CRANBERRY SQUARES

ADD THIS GOODIE TO YOUR HOLIDAY BAKING LIST.

CRUST

½ CUP COLD BUTTER	125 mL
¼ CUP SUGAR	60 mL
1 CUP FLOUR	250 mL

FILLING

1½ CUPS FROZEN CRANBERRIES	375 mL
¼ CUP PACKED BROWN SUGAR	60 mL
2 EGGS	
1 CUP FIRMLY PACKED BROWN SUGAR	250 mL
1 TSP. VANILLA	5 mL
⅓ CUP FLOUR	75 mL
½ TSP. BAKING POWDER	2 mL
¼ TSP. SALT	1 mL

TO MAKE CRUST: CUT BUTTER INTO SUGAR AND FLOUR UNTIL CRUMBLY (A FOOD PROCESSOR DOES A DANDY JOB). PAT INTO AN 8" SQUARE PAN. BAKE AT 350°F FOR 15 TO 20 MINUTES OR UNTIL GOLDEN.

TO MAKE FILLING: IN A SAUCEPAN, COOK CRANBERRIES (DON'T BOTHER TO THAW) AND ¼ CUP BROWN SUGAR OVER MEDIUM-LOW HEAT UNTIL BERRIES ARE SOFTENED AND THE SKINS POP, ABOUT 10 MINUTES. COOL. IN A LARGE BOWL, BEAT EGGS AND GRADUALLY ADD BROWN SUGAR. BEAT UNTIL THICKENED. BEAT IN VANILLA.

CRANBERRY SQUARES

THIS RECIPE CONTINUED FROM PAGE 176

COMBINE DRY INGREDIENTS AND ADD TO EGG MIXTURE. STIR IN COOLED CRANBERRIES AND SPREAD MIXTURE OVER CRUST. BAKE AT 350°F FOR 35-40 MINUTES. DON'T OVERBAKE.

NO MAN WAS EVER SHOT WHILE DOING THE DISHES.

CHOCOLATE CARAMEL SQUARES

WHAT A WAY TO EAT YOUR CEREAL!!

¾ CUP MARGARINE	175 mL
4 - 2½ OZ. MARS BARS, CUT IN CHUNKS	4 - 66 g
6 CUPS CORNFLAKES, CRUSHED	1.5 L
1 CUP SEMI-SWEET CHOCOLATE CHIPS	250 mL

IN A LARGE POT PARTIALLY MELT MARGARINE. ADD CHOCOLATE BAR CHUNKS AND MELT OVER LOW HEAT, STIRRING CONSTANTLY, UNTIL MIXTURE IS SMOOTH. POUR CORNFLAKES INTO MIXTURE AND BLEND WELL. PRESS INTO A 9" X 13" PAN. MELT CHOCOLATE CHIPS AND SPREAD OVER TOP. THIS RECIPE CAN ALSO BE MADE IN THE MICROWAVE.

CHOCOLATE PECAN BARS

THESE ARE VERY RICH AND CHEWY.

CRUST

2 CUPS FLOUR	500 mL
½ CUP WHITE SUGAR	125 mL
⅔ CUP BUTTER	150 mL

FILLING

6 - 1 OZ. SQUARES SEMI-SWEET CHOCOLATE	170 g
1½ CUPS LIGHT CORN SYRUP	375 mL
1½ CUPS WHITE SUGAR	375 mL
4 EGGS, SLIGHTLY BEATEN	
1½ TSP. VANILLA	7 mL
2 CUPS CHOPPED PECANS	500 mL

TOPPING (OPTIONAL)

2 TBSP. BUTTER	30 mL
2 - 1 OZ. SQUARES SEMI-SWEET CHOCOLATE	55 g

TO MAKE CRUST: COMBINE INGREDIENTS AND MIX TO COARSE, CRUMBLE STAGE. PAT FIRMLY INTO GREASED 10" X 15" EDGED COOKIE SHEET. BAKE AT 350°F FOR 15 MINUTES.

TO MAKE FILLING: HEAT CHOCOLATE AND CORN SYRUP OVER LOW HEAT UNTIL CHOCOLATE IS MELTED. REMOVE FROM HEAT, ADD SUGAR, EGGS AND VANILLA, MIXING WELL. STIR IN PECANS. SPREAD OVER HOT CRUST. BAKE AT 350°F FOR 25-30 MINUTES, OR UNTIL FILLING IS FIRM AROUND EDGES AND SLIGHTLY SOFT IN CENTER. COOL ON A RACK.

CHOCOLATE PECAN BARS

THIS RECIPE CONTINUED FROM PAGE 178.

TO MAKE TOPPING: MELT BUTTER AND CHOCOLATE IN PAN AT LOW HEAT AND DRIZZLE OVER TOP. CUT INTO SMALL RECTANGLES WHILE STILL WARM BUT LEAVE IN PAN UNTIL COOLED.

GOURMET: A FRENCH WORD MEANING 400% MARK UP.

PUFFED WHEAT SQUARES

EDITH BROUGHT THIS BACK FROM LONGVIEW WHERE SHE LIVED FOR MANY YEARS.

½ CUP MARGARINE	125 mL
1 CUP CORN SYRUP	250 mL
1 CUP WHITE SUGAR	250 mL
¼ CUP BROWN SUGAR	60 mL
6 HEAPING TBSP. COCOA	90 mL
1 TSP. VANILLA	5 mL
10 CUPS PUFFED WHEAT	2.5 L

COMBINE MARGARINE, CORN SYRUP, SUGARS AND COCOA IN HEAVY SAUCEPAN. BRING TO BOIL. REMOVE FROM HEAT AND ADD VANILLA. POUR OVER PUFFED WHEAT. MIX WELL AND PRESS INTO A GREASED 9" X 13" PAN. MAKES 24 SQUARES.

RASPBERRY PECAN TART WITH SOUR CREAM GLAZE

THIS IS SO EASY - AND SO ELEGANT. A "WINNER" FOR THE NEXT SPECIAL OCCASION!

FLAKY LEMON PASTRY CRUST

1 CUP FLOUR	250 mL
½ TSP. BAKING POWDER	2 mL
¼ CUP SUGAR	60 mL
½ CUP BUTTER	125 mL
1 EGG	
1 TBSP. GRATED LEMON PEEL	15 mL

FILLING

1 CUP RASPBERRY JAM	250 mL
½ CUP FINELY CHOPPED PECANS	125 mL
½ CUP BUTTER	125 mL
¾ CUP SUGAR	175 mL
2 EGGS	
1 TSP. VANILLA	5 mL
1 TBSP. GRATED LEMON PEEL	15 mL
1 CUP FINELY CHOPPED PECANS	250 mL

GLAZE

1 TBSP. SOUR CREAM	15 mL
1 TSP. VANILLA	5 mL
⅔ CUP ICING SUGAR	150 mL

TO MAKE CRUST: MIX TOGETHER FLOUR, BAKING POWDER AND SUGAR. CUT IN BUTTER UNTIL MIXTURE RESEMBLES COARSE MEAL. BEAT IN THE EGG AND LEMON PEEL UNTIL JUST

RASPBERRY PECAN TART
WITH SOUR CREAM GLAZE

THIS RECIPE CONTINUED FROM PAGE 180.

BLENDED. DO NOT OVERMIX. PAT DOUGH ONTO THE BOTTOM OF A GREASED 10" SPRINGFORM PAN AND BAKE AT 350°F FOR 25 MINUTES, OR UNTIL TOP IS LIGHTLY BROWNED. ALLOW CRUST TO COOL.

TO MAKE FILLING: STIR TOGETHER RASPBERRY JAM AND PECANS AND SPREAD EVENLY OVER THE CRUST. BEAT BUTTER AND SUGAR UNTIL CREAMY. ADD EGGS, ONE AT A TIME, BEATING WELL AFTER EACH ADDITION. STIR IN VANILLA, LEMON PEEL AND PECANS UNTIL BLENDED. POUR NUT MIXTURE OVER THE JAM. BAKE AT 350°F FOR 40 MINUTES, OR UNTIL FILLING IS SET. COOL.

TO MAKE GLAZE: STIR TOGETHER SOUR CREAM, VANILLA AND ICING SUGAR AND DRIZZLE OVER TART. SERVES 8-10 LUCKY PEOPLE!

PLAYING CARDS CAN BE EXPENSIVE - SO CAN ANY GAME WHERE YOU ARE HOLDING HANDS.

CHOCOLATE BRITTLE PIE

CRUST

2 CUPS CHOCOLATE WAFER CRUMBS	500 mL
½ CUP SUGAR	125 mL
½ CUP MELTED BUTTER	125 mL

FILLING

2 QTS. VANILLA ICE CREAM	2 L
½ LB. PEANUT BRITTLE CANDY	250 g
2 CUPS CHOCOLATE CHIPS	500 mL

TOPPING

½ CUP WHIPPING CREAM, WHIPPED	125 mL
½ CUP CHOCOLATE SAUCE	125 mL

PREHEAT OVEN TO 300°F. COMBINE CRUST INGREDIENTS AND PAT INTO A 9" PIE PLATE. BAKE FOR 20 MINUTES. COOL CRUST COMPLETELY. SOFTEN ICE CREAM. FINELY CRUSH PEANUT BRITTLE. STIR BRITTLE AND CHOCOLATE CHIPS INTO SOFTENED ICE CREAM. SPOON ONTO CRUST AND PACK WELL. COVER AND REFREEZE UNTIL ICE CREAM IS HARD. SERVE WITH WHIPPED CREAM AND DRIZZLE WITH CHOCOLATE SAUCE. SERVES 8.

EVE ASKED ADAM, "DO YOU LOVE ME?"
HIS REPLY, "WHO ELSE?"

RHUBARB STRAWBERRY CRUMBLE PIE

THE FIRST SIGNS OF SPRING ARE BAKED INTO THIS PIE.

1¼ CUPS SUGAR	300 mL
¼ CUP FLOUR	60 mL
1 CUP PLAIN YOGURT OR SOUR CREAM	250 mL
3½ CUPS DICED RHUBARB	825 L
1½ CUPS SLICED STRAWBERRIES	375 mL
10" UNBAKED PASTRY SHELL	25 cm
½ CUP PACKED BROWN SUGAR	125 mL
½ CUP FLOUR	125 mL
¼ CUP COLD BUTTER	60 mL

PREHEAT OVEN TO 450°F. IN A LARGE BOWL, COMBINE SUGAR, FLOUR, YOGURT, RHUBARB AND STRAWBERRIES. SPOON INTO UNBAKED PIE SHELL. IN A SMALL BOWL, MIX TOGETHER BROWN SUGAR AND FLOUR. CUT IN THE BUTTER UNTIL THE MIXTURE IS CRUMBLY. SPRINKLE ON TOP OF THE PIE. BAKE FOR 15 MINUTES. REDUCE HEAT TO 350°F AND CONTINUE BAKING FOR ANOTHER 30 MINUTES. SERVE HOT OR COLD.

A WISE MAN NEVER LAUGHS AT HIS WIFE'S OLD CLOTHES.

FROZEN PEANUT BUTTER PIE

A REAL SMOOTHIE . . . FOR YOUR SQUIRRELY FRIENDS.

CRUST

1/3 CUP BUTTER	75 mL
6 OZ. PKG. SEMI-SWEET CHOCOLATE CHIPS	170 g
2 1/2 CUPS RICE KRISPIES CEREAL	625 mL

FILLING

8 OZ. PKG. CREAM CHEESE, SOFTENED	250 g
10 OZ. CAN SWEETENED CONDENSED MILK	284 mL
3/4 CUP PEANUT BUTTER	175 mL
2 TBSP. LEMON JUICE	30 mL
1 TSP. VANILLA	5 mL
1 CUP WHIPPING CREAM, WHIPPED	250 mL

CHOCOLATE FUDGE SAUCE

IN HEAVY SAUCEPAN, MELT BUTTER AND CHOCOLATE CHIPS OVER LOW HEAT. REMOVE FROM HEAT AND GENTLY STIR IN CEREAL UNTIL COMPLETELY COATED. PRESS INTO BOTTOM AND SIDES OF A BUTTERED 9" PIE PLATE. CHILL 30 MINUTES.

IN LARGE BOWL, BEAT CHEESE UNTIL FLUFFY. GRADUALLY BEAT IN CONDENSED MILK AND PEANUT BUTTER UNTIL SMOOTH. STIR IN LEMON JUICE AND VANILLA. FOLD IN WHIPPED CREAM. POUR INTO PREPARED CRUST. DRIZZLE CHOCOLATE TOPPING OVER PIE AND FREEZE 4 HOURS, OR UNTIL FIRM. IF YOU HAVE ANY LEFTOVERS, WRAP AND RETURN TO FREEZER.

FROZEN LEMON PUFF

GUARANTEED RAVES AND A GREAT MAKE AHEAD.

5 EGGS (SEPARATE 3 AND RESERVE WHITES)	
3/4 CUP LEMON JUICE	175 mL
1 CUP SUGAR	250 mL
2 CUPS WHIPPING CREAM	500 mL
VANILLA WAFERS TO COVER BOTTOM AND SIDES OF PAN	
DASH CREAM OF TARTAR	
1/4 CUP ICING SUGAR	60 mL

MIX 2 EGGS AND 3 EGG YOLKS, LEMON JUICE AND SUGAR TOGETHER IN THE TOP OF A DOUBLE BOILER AND COOK UNTIL THICK, STIRRING CONSTANTLY. COOL. WHIP THE CREAM AND FOLD INTO LEMON MIXTURE. LINE SIDES AND BOTTOM OF A 9" SPRINGFORM PAN WITH VANILLA WAFERS. POUR LEMON MIXTURE INTO THE PAN. BEAT THE 3 EGG WHITES UNTIL FOAMY. ADD CREAM OF TARTAR AND ICING SUGAR AND BEAT UNTIL PEAKS ARE STIFF. SPREAD ON THE LEMON MIXTURE AND BROWN UNDER THE BROILER. (WATCH CAREFULLY!) COVER WITH FOIL MAKING SURE IT DOESN'T TOUCH THE MERINGUE. FREEZE 8 HOURS OR MORE. REMOVE FROM FREEZER (TAKING FOIL OFF IMMEDIATELY) AT LEAST 1½ HOURS BEFORE SERVING. SERVES 10-12.

MAKE IT AHEAD. YOU'LL WANT TO STEAL SPOONFULS BEFORE SERVING TIME.

CRUST

1½ CUPS CRUSHED CHOCOLATE WAFERS	375 mL
¼ CUP BUTTER	60 mL
¾ CUP CRUSHED PECANS OR ALMONDS	175 mL

MOUSSE

¾ CUP CHOCOLATE CHIPS	175 mL
8 OZ. CREAM CHEESE	250 g
¼ CUP SUGAR	60 mL
1 TSP. VANILLA	5 mL
2 EGGS, SEPARATED	
¼ CUP SUGAR	60 mL
1 CUP WHIPPING CREAM	250 mL

CHOCOLATE CURLS

TO MAKE CRUST: PREHEAT OVEN TO 325°F. COMBINE CHOCOLATE CRUMBS AND BUTTER AND PRESS INTO A 9" SPRINGFORM PAN. SPRINKLE NUTS OVER TOP OF CRUST AND BAKE FOR 10 MINUTES.

TO MAKE MOUSSE: MELT CHOCOLATE CHIPS AND SET ASIDE TO COOL. BLEND CREAM CHEESE, SUGAR AND VANILLA. BEAT EGG YOLKS, ADD AND STIR. MIX IN COOLED CHOCOLATE.

BEAT EGG WHITES UNTIL SOFT PEAKS FORM. ADD SUGAR SLOWLY AND BEAT UNTIL STIFF. FOLD INTO CHOCOLATE MIXTURE. WHIP CREAM AND

ACES

THIS RECIPE CONTINUED FROM PAGE 186.

FOLD INTO THE CHOCOLATE MOUSSE. POUR INTO SPRINGFORM PAN. COVER AND PLACE IN FREEZER OVERNIGHT. REMOVE FROM FREEZER AND REFRIGERATE 5 HOURS BEFORE SERVING. REMOVE FROM PAN AND GARNISH WITH CHOCOLATE CURLS. SERVES 8-10.
(SEE PICTURE - PAGE 173.)

CHANTILLY L'ORANGE

A MELT-IN-YOUR-MOUTH MAKE AHEAD. SECOND HELPS??

MERINGUE

3 EGG WHITES, AT ROOM TEMPERATURE	
1¼ CUPS ICING SUGAR	300 mL

FILLING

2 CUPS WHIPPING CREAM	500 mL
2 TBSP. GRAND MARNIER OR ORANGE LIQUEUR	30 mL
2 TBSP. FINELY GRATED ORANGE PEEL	30 mL

CHOCOLATE SAUCE

4 - 1 OZ. SQUARES SEMI-SWEET CHOCOLATE	115 g
2 TBSP. MARGARINE	30 mL
2 TBSP. ICING SUGAR	30 mL
3 TBSP. WATER	45 mL
1 TBSP. GRAND MARNIER	15 mL

THIS RECIPE IS CONTINUED ON PAGE 188.

CHANTILLY L'ORANGE

THIS RECIPE CONTINUED FROM PAGE 187.

TO MAKE MERINGUE: PREHEAT OVEN TO 275°F. BEAT EGG WHITES UNTIL VERY STIFF. SPRINKLE ICING SUGAR OVER WHITES AND FOLD IN WITH A SPATULA. SPREAD ONTO A FOIL-COVERED COOKIE SHEET TO ONE INCH THICKNESS AND BAKE FOR ONE HOUR. TURN OFF OVEN AND COOL IN OPEN OVEN FOR AT LEAST ONE HOUR. BREAK INTO ONE-INCH CHUNKS.

TO MAKE FILLING: BEAT CREAM UNTIL THICK AND ADD GRAND MARNIER AND ORANGE PEEL. MIX WELL. FOLD IN MERINGUE PIECES. TRANSFER TO A MOLD OR PRETTY GLASS BOWL. COVER AND FREEZE.

TO MAKE CHOCOLATE SAUCE: MELT CHOCOLATE AND MARGARINE IN MICROWAVE OR DOUBLE BOILER. (WATCH CLOSELY IF USING THE MICROWAVE AS CHOCOLATE CAN BURN QUICKLY.) DO NOT BOIL! ADD REMAINING INGREDIENTS AND BLEND WELL. ADD MORE WATER IF SAUCE BECOMES TOO THICK. SERVE WARM CHOCOLATE SAUCE OVER FROZEN CHANTILLY. SERVES 6.

NOBODY CARES HOW BAD YOUR ENGLISH IS, AS LONG AS YOUR SCOTCH IS GOOD.

UPSIDE-DOWN CHOCOLATE FUDGE PUDDING

A GREAT WINTER DESSERT - THE SAUCE ENDS UP ON THE BOTTOM AND THE CAKE ON TOP!

1 CUP FLOUR	250 mL
2 TSP. BAKING POWDER	10 mL
3/4 CUP SUGAR	175 mL
1/2 TSP. SALT	2 mL
3 TBSP. COCOA	45 mL
1/2 CUP MILK	125 mL
2 TBSP. MARGARINE, MELTED	30 mL
1/4 CUP CHOPPED PECANS (OPTIONAL)	60 mL
3/4 CUP BROWN SUGAR	175 mL
1/2 CUP COCOA	125 mL
2 CUPS BOILING WATER.	500 mL

PREHEAT OVEN TO 350°F. MIX FLOUR, BAKING POWDER, SUGAR, SALT AND COCOA TOGETHER. COMBINE MILK AND MELTED MARGARINE. ADD TO DRY INGREDIENTS TO FORM A STIFF MIXTURE. ADD NUTS IF DESIRED. PUT INTO A GREASED 8" X 8" BAKING PAN. COMBINE BROWN SUGAR, COCOA AND BOILING WATER. POUR OVER BATTER AND BAKE FOR 40 MINUTES. SERVE WARM WITH A BIG SCOOP OF VANILLA ICE CREAM OR ORANGE SHERBET. SERVES 4-6.

PESSIMIST'S DEN: ROOM FOR DOUBT.

CAJUN BREAD PUDDING
WITH RUM SAUCE AND SOFT CREAM

THIS IS UNBELIEVABLY GOOD!! A MUST TO TRY. IT'S AMAZING WHAT A LITTLE BOOZE CAN DO FOR BREAD. (SEE PICTURE OPPOSITE.)

PUDDING

⅓ CUP BUTTER OR MARGARINE, MELTED	75 mL
16 CUPS FRENCH BREAD CUBES, DAY OLD, LIGHTLY PACKED	4 L
3 EGGS	
1½ CUPS SUGAR	375 mL
2 TBSP. VANILLA	30 mL
1 TSP. NUTMEG	5 mL
1½ TSP. CINNAMON	7 mL
3 CUPS MILK	750 mL
¾ CUP GOLDEN RAISINS	175 mL
1 CUP CHOPPED TOASTED PECANS	250 mL

RUM SAUCE

1 CUP BUTTER OR MARGARINE	250 mL
1½ CUPS SUGAR	375 mL
2 EGGS, BEATEN UNTIL FROTHY	
¼–½ CUP DARK RUM	60–125 mL

SOFT CREAM

2 CUPS WHIPPING CREAM	500 mL
⅓ CUP ICING SUGAR	75 mL
1 TBSP. VANILLA	15 mL
2 TBSP. BRANDY	30 mL
2 TBSP. FRANGELICO LIQUEUR	30 mL
¼ CUP SOUR CREAM	60 mL

THIS RECIPE IS CONTINUED ON PAGE 193.

PICTURED ON OVERLEAF

CAJUN BREAD PUDDING WITH RUM
SAUCE AND SOFT CREAM - PAGE 190

CAJUN BREAD PUDDING
WITH RUM SAUCE AND SOFT CREAM

THIS RECIPE CONTINUED FROM PAGE 190.

TO MAKE PUDDING: POUR A SMALL AMOUNT OF THE MELTED BUTTER IN A 9" X 13" PAN AND SWIRL AROUND TO COVER BOTTOM AND SIDES. PLACE BREAD CUBES IN PAN. IN A LARGE BOWL, BEAT EGGS AND SUGAR UNTIL THICKENED (3-4 MINUTES). ADD VANILLA, NUTMEG, CINNAMON AND MILK PLUS RESERVED BUTTER. BEAT AT LOW SPEED TO COMBINE. STIR IN RAISINS AND PECANS. POUR OVER BREAD. STIR TO EVENLY DISTRIBUTE RAISINS AND NUTS. ALLOW BREAD TO ABSORB ALL LIQUID (30 - 45 MINUTES). PRESS BREAD DOWN OFTEN TO COVER ALL CUBES. PREHEAT OVEN TO 350°. BAKE UNTIL CRUSTY AND GOLDEN BROWN (45-60 MINUTES). COOL TO LUKEWARM AND SLICE INTO SQUARES.

TO MAKE RUM SAUCE: CREAM BUTTER AND SUGAR UNTIL LIGHT AND FLUFFY. PUT IN TOP OF A DOUBLE BOILER OVER SIMMERING WATER. COOK 20 MINUTES, WHISKING OFTEN. IN A BOWL, WHISK 2 TBSP. BUTTER-SUGAR MIXTURE INTO BEATEN EGGS, THEN WHISK IN 2 TBSP. MORE. NOW, WHISK EGG MIXTURE INTO BUTTER/SUGAR MIXTURE. COOK OVER SIMMERING WATER 4-5 MINUTES, WHISKING CONSTANTLY. COOL SLIGHTLY. WHISK IN RUM. (BY NOW YOU'RE PROBABLY ALL WHISKED OUT - TASTE THE SAUCE AND YOU'LL KNOW IT WAS WORTH IT!)

THIS RECIPE IS CONTINUED ON PAGE 194.

CAJUN BREAD PUDDING WITH RUM SAUCE AND SOFT CREAM

THIS RECIPE CONTINUED FROM PAGE 193.

TO MAKE SOFT CREAM: CHILL BEATERS AND A MEDIUM-SIZED BOWL UNTIL VERY COLD. BEAT INGREDIENTS ON MEDIUM-HIGH UNTIL SOFT PEAKS FORM (3-4 MINUTES). DO NOT OVERBEAT. COVER TIGHTLY AND REFRIGERATE UNTIL SERVED.

TO SERVE: ON INDIVIDUAL PLATES, PLACE A SPOONFUL OF WARM RUM SAUCE, A SQUARE OF PUDDING AND A LARGE DOLLOP OF SOFT CREAM. AT THIS POINT, GUESTS WILL BE INCLINED TO EXCLAIM, "DON'T Y'ALL JUST LUUUVE THIS?!!" SERVES 12-14.

BEFORE YOU TELL A MAN YOU LOVE HIS COMPANY, MAKE SURE HE OWNS IT.

JAKE'S RICE PUDDING

COMFORT FOOD. AN OLD-TIME FAVORITE - BUT THEN, SO IS JAKE.

1⅓ CUPS MILK	325 mL
½ CUP BROWN SUGAR	125 mL
1 TBSP. BUTTER	15 mL
1 TSP. VANILLA	5 mL
2 EGGS, BEATEN	
1 TSP. LEMON JUICE	5 mL
⅓-½ CUP RAISINS	75-125 mL
2 CUPS COOKED RICE	500 mL
CINNAMON OR NUTMEG TO TASTE	

PREHEAT OVEN TO 325°F. COMBINE MILK, SUGAR, BUTTER, VANILLA, EGGS, LEMON JUICE AND RAISINS. MIX WELL AND ADD TO RICE. POUR INTO A GREASED 2-QUART BAKING DISH AND COVER. BAKE FOR 45-55 MINUTES, UNTIL PUDDING IS SET. SERVES 4-6.

IF YOU WANT TO GET FANCY WITH THIS OLD-FASHIONED FAVORITE - POUR WHIPPING CREAM SPIKED WITH RUM OVER INDIVIDUAL SERVINGS.

AGE IS A MATTER OF THE MIND - IF YOU DON'T MIND, IT DOESN'T MATTER.

WHITE CHOCOLATE MOUSSE WITH RASPBERRY SAUCE

MOUSSE

6 OZ. WHITE CHOCOLATE (BULK IS BEST)	170 g
½ CUP MILK, WARMED	125 mL
1 PKG. GELATIN, 1 TBSP.	15 mL
1 TSP. VANILLA	5 mL
2 EGG WHITES	
1 CUP WHIPPING CREAM	250 mL
1 TSP. LEMON JUICE	5 mL

RASPBERRY SAUCE

15 OZ. PKG. FROZEN RASPBERRIES WITH JUICE	425 mL
JUICE OF ½ LEMON	
½ CUP SUGAR	125 mL
2 TSP. CORNSTARCH	10 mL
¼ CUP FRAMBOISE, KIRSCH OR GRAND MARNIER	60 mL

TO MAKE MOUSSE: MELT CHOCOLATE WITH ¼ CUP OF THE MILK. (IN DOUBLE BOILER OR AT LOW HEAT IN MICROWAVE.) STIR UNTIL SMOOTH AND SET ASIDE. ADD GELATIN TO REMAINING ¼ CUP OF WARMED MILK AND STIR UNTIL DISSOLVED. ADD GELATIN MIXTURE AND VANILLA TO CHOCOLATE AND MIX UNTIL SMOOTH. COOL TO ROOM TEMPERATURE. BEAT EGG WHITES UNTIL STIFF AND FOLD INTO CHOCOLATE MIXTURE A LITTLE AT A TIME. WHIP CREAM UNTIL STIFF. FOLD CREAM AND LEMON JUICE INTO CHOCOLATE

WHITE CHOCOLATE MOUSSE WITH RASPBERRY SAUCE

THIS RECIPE CONTINUED FROM PAGE 196.

MIXTURE. POUR INTO SERVING BOWL CHILL UNTIL FIRM, AT LEAST 2 HOURS.

TO MAKE SAUCE: COMBINE THAWED RASPBERRIES AND JUICE WITH LEMON JUICE IN BLENDER. PURÉE UNTIL SMOOTH AND STRAIN TO REMOVE ALL SEEDS. POUR RASPBERRY MIXTURE INTO SAUCEPAN AND ADD SUGAR. BRING TO BOIL OVER MEDIUM-HIGH HEAT, THEN SIMMER FOR 15 MINUTES. DISSOLVE CORNSTARCH IN LIQUEUR AND STIR INTO RASPBERRY MIXTURE. REMOVE FROM HEAT AND COOL. COVER AND REFRIGERATE. TO SERVE, SPOON SAUCE ONTO A GLASS PLATE AND TOP WITH A LARGE SPOONFUL OF MOUSSE. SERVES 4-6.

MANY A DUMB BLONDE IS REALLY A SMART BRUNETTE.

BLUEBERRY BUCKLE

DOWN HOME DELICIOUS!

BATTER

1 CUP FLOUR	250 mL
1½ TSP. BAKING POWDER	7 mL
PINCH OF SALT	
¼ CUP BUTTER	60 mL
½ CUP SUGAR	125 mL
1 EGG	
½ CUP MILK	125 mL
2 CUPS FRESH OR FROZEN BLUEBERRIES	500 mL

TOPPING

⅓ CUP BROWN SUGAR	75 mL
½ CUP FLOUR	125 mL
1 TSP. CINNAMON	5 mL
¼ CUP BUTTER OR MARGARINE	60 mL

TO MAKE BATTER: PREHEAT OVEN TO 400°F. IF USING FROZEN BLUEBERRIES, DO NOT THAW. MIX FLOUR, BAKING POWDER AND SALT IN A SMALL BOWL. BEAT BUTTER AND SUGAR UNTIL LIGHT AND FLUFFY, THEN BEAT IN EGG. MIX IN HALF THE FLOUR MIXTURE, FOLLOWED BY MILK. ADD REMAINING FLOUR MIXTURE AND MIX UNTIL COMBINED. POUR BATTER INTO A GREASED 8" BAKING PAN. SPRINKLE WITH BLUEBERRIES. PREPARE TOPPING IMMEDIATELY.

TO MAKE TOPPING: MIX DRY INGREDIENTS IN A MEDIUM-SIZED BOWL. USING 2 KNIVES OR PASTRY

BLUEBERRY BUCKLE

THIS RECIPE CONTINUED FROM PAGE 198.

CUTTER, CUT IN BUTTER UNTIL MIXTURE RESEMBLES COARSE MEAL. SPRINKLE OVER BLUEBERRIES. BAKE ON MIDDLE RACK OF OVEN FOR 45 MINUTES. COOL 10 MINUTES. CUT INTO SQUARES AND SERVE WARM WITH WHIPPED CREAM OR VANILLA ICE CREAM. SERVES 6.

FRESH STRAWBERRY SHERBET

DEFINITELY A FROZEN ASSET!

2/3 CUP SUGAR	150 mL
2/3 CUP WATER	150 mL
5 CUPS STRAWBERRIES, PURÉED & CHILLED	1.25 L
2 TBSP. GRAND MARNIER	30 mL
2 TBSP. LEMON JUICE	30 mL
ZEST OF 1 LEMON	

COMBINE SUGAR AND WATER IN SAUCEPAN OVER MEDIUM HEAT AND STIR UNTIL SUGAR IS DISSOLVED. COOL AND CHILL. COMBINE PURÉED STRAWBERRIES, GRAND MARNIER, LEMON JUICE AND LEMON ZEST AND BLEND WELL. ADD SUGAR SYRUP TO STRAWBERRY MIXTURE. FREEZE IN AN 8" SQUARE METAL PAN. AFTER MIXTURE IS FROZEN, ABOUT 3 HOURS, PARTIALLY THAW AND BEAT IN A FOOD PROCESSOR. THIS BREAKS DOWN THE ICE CRYSTALS AND GIVES IT A FLUFFY TEXTURE. REFREEZE FOR AT LEAST 3 HOURS. SERVES 4.

BLUEBERRY BONANZA

YOU'VE GOT IT - ANOTHER EASY DESSERT GUARANTEED TO PLEASE.

CRUST

1 SLEEVE OF DIGESTIVE BISCUITS, ABOUT 27, FINELY CRUSHED (GRAHAM WAFERS WOULD BE A GOOD SUBSTITUTE)	
1 TSP. SUGAR	5 mL
1/4 TSP. CINNAMON	1 mL
1/2 CUP BUTTER	125 mL

CHEESE LAYER

8 OZ. CREAM CHEESE	250 g
1/2 CUP SUGAR	125 mL
2 EGGS	
1 TSP. VANILLA	5 mL

BLUEBERRY LAYER

3 CUPS FROZEN BLUEBERRIES	750 mL
1/2 CUP SUGAR	125 mL
1/2 CUP WATER	125 mL
1 TBSP. LEMON JUICE	15 mL
4 TSP. CORNSTARCH	20 mL
1/2 CUP COLD WATER	125 mL
2 CUPS WHIPPING CREAM	500 mL
2 TBSP. SUGAR	30 mL
3 DIGESTIVE BISCUITS, CRUSHED	

TO MAKE CRUST: MIX INGREDIENTS TOGETHER AND PAT LIGHTLY INTO A 9" X 13" PAN AND

BLUEBERRY BONANZA

THIS RECIPE CONTINUED FROM PAGE 200.

BAKE AT 325° F FOR 10 MINUTES.

TO MAKE CHEESE LAYER: MIX INGREDIENTS TOGETHER AND SPREAD OVER CRUST. BAKE AT 325°F FOR 20 MINUTES.

TO MAKE BLUEBERRY LAYER: COMBINE BLUEBERRIES, SUGAR, WATER AND LEMON JUICE IN A SAUCEPAN AND BRING TO A BOIL. DISSOLVE CORNSTARCH IN THE COLD WATER AND ADD TO THE BLUEBERRY MIXTURE. STIR UNTIL THICKENED AND POUR OVER BAKED CHEESE LAYER. COOL COMPLETELY.

WHIP CREAM WITH SUGAR AND SPREAD ON TOP OF BLUEBERRY LAYER. SPRINKLE WITH DIGESTIVE BISCUIT CRUMBS AND REFRIGERATE UNTIL SERVING TIME. IF YOU MAKE THIS THE NIGHT BEFORE - DON'T WHIP THE CREAM UNTIL JUST BEFORE SERVING. SERVES 10-12.

AGE IS NOT AN IMPROVEMENT UNLESS YOU'RE A CHEESE.

FRESH BERRY TART

Now here's a tart you'd love to have at your table. A great make ahead.

CRUST

1 cup flour	250 mL
½ cup icing sugar	125 mL
2 tbsp. lemon rind	30 mL
½ cup butter	125 mL
2 tbsp. lemon juice	30 mL

CUSTARD

⅓ cup sugar	75 mL
1 egg	
1 egg yolk	
2 tbsp. cornstarch	30 mL
1½ tbsp. flour	22 mL
1 cup milk	250 mL
1 tsp. vanilla	5 mL
4 cups fresh berries (use any combination of blueberries, raspberries or sliced strawberries)	1 L

GLAZE

½ cup raspberry or apple jelly, melted	125 mL

TO MAKE CRUST: Combine flour, sugar and rind. Cut in butter until mixture resembles coarse crumbs. Gradually add lemon juice, stirring with a fork until mixture is gathered into a ball. Wrap and

FRESH BERRY TART

THIS RECIPE CONTINUED FROM PAGE 202.

REFRIGERATE FOR 30 MINUTES. ROLL DOUGH OUT TO FORM AN 11" CIRCLE. TRANSFER TO 9" TART OR FLAN PAN WITH REMOVABLE BOTTOM, PRESSING INTO BOTTOM AND SIDES. CHILL AGAIN FOR 30 MINUTES. PREHEAT OVEN TO 425°F. PRICK BOTTOM AND SIDES OF PASTRY WITH FORK TO PREVENT SHRINKAGE. BAKE 10 MINUTES AT 425°F, THEN REDUCE HEAT TO 350°F FOR THE LAST 8-10 MINUTES, OR UNTIL GOLDEN.

TO MAKE CUSTARD: WHISK SUGAR, EGG AND EGG YOLK UNTIL THICK. ADD CORNSTARCH AND FLOUR AND WHISK WELL. HEAT MILK AND VANILLA IN A SAUCEPAN UNTIL ALMOST BOILING. GRADUALLY ADD MILK TO EGG MIXTURE, THEN RETURN TO SAUCEPAN. COOK OVER LOW HEAT, WHISKING CONSTANTLY UNTIL MIXTURE BOILS AND THICKENS. TRANSFER TO BOWL AND REFRIGERATE UNTIL WELL-CHILLED. (THIS CAN BE PREPARED A DAY AHEAD.)

TO ASSEMBLE: REMOVE CRUST FROM TART PAN AND SET ON PLATTER. SPREAD COOLED CUSTARD OVER BOTTOM OF CRUST AND ARRANGE FRESH BERRIES ON TOP. GENTLY BRUSH MELTED JELLY OVER FRUIT. CHILL UNTIL SERVING TIME. SERVES 10-12. (SEE PICTURE - PAGE 173.)

PECAN HOLIDAY CAKE

ANOTHER ONE OF THOSE GREAT BRUNCH, BUNDT, BEDAZZLEMENTS.

2 CUPS BUTTER, SOFTENED	500 mL
2 CUPS SUGAR	500 mL
6 EGGS	
1 TSP. GRATED LEMON PEEL	5 mL
1 TBSP. LEMON JUICE	15 mL
1 TBSP. VANILLA	15 mL
1½ CUPS GOLDEN SEEDLESS RAISINS	375 mL
4 CUPS CHOPPED PECANS	1 L
3 CUPS FLOUR	750 mL
¼ TSP. SALT	1 mL
1 TSP. BAKING POWDER	5 mL

GLAZE

¼ CUP ORANGE JUICE	60 mL
¼ CUP LEMON JUICE	60 mL
¼ CUP SUGAR	60 mL

CREAM BUTTER AND SUGAR UNTIL FLUFFY. ADD EGGS, ONE AT A TIME, BEATING WELL AFTER EACH ADDITION. STIR IN LEMON PEEL, LEMON JUICE AND VANILLA. COMBINE RAISINS, PECANS AND ¼ CUP OF THE FLOUR. COMBINE REMAINING FLOUR, SALT AND BAKING POWDER. FOLD INTO CREAMED MIXTURE ALTERNATING WITH NUT MIXTURE. SPOON BATTER INTO A GREASED AND FLOURED 10" BUNDT PAN. BAKE AT 300°F FOR ABOUT 1½ HOURS, OR UNTIL AN INSERTED TOOTHPICK COMES OUT CLEAN. COOL SLIGHTLY AND REMOVE FROM PAN.

PECAN HOLIDAY CAKE

THIS RECIPE CONTINUED FROM PAGE 204.

FOR GLAZE: COMBINE ALL INGREDIENTS AND HEAT, STIRRING CONSTANTLY, UNTIL SUGAR IS DISSOLVED. POUR OVER WARM CAKE. DUST LIGHTLY WITH ICING SUGAR IF DESIRED. THIS FREEZES WELL.

RHUBARB COBBLER

4 CUPS RHUBARB, CUT IN ½" PIECES	1 L
¾-1 CUP SUGAR	175-250 mL
1¼ CUPS FLOUR	300 mL
3 TBSP. SUGAR	45 mL
1 TBSP. BAKING POWDER	15 mL
¼ TSP. SALT	1 mL
⅓ CUP MARGARINE	75 mL
1 EGG, BEATEN	
½ CUP MILK	125 mL

PREHEAT OVEN TO 375°F. COMBINE RHUBARB AND SUGAR AND PLACE IN A SHALLOW, GREASED 9" CASSEROLE. TO MAKE BATTER, COMBINE FLOUR, SUGAR, BAKING POWDER AND SALT, THEN CUT IN MARGARINE. COMBINE BEATEN EGG AND MILK AND ADD TO DRY INGREDIENTS. STIR WITH FORK TO MAKE A STIFF BATTER. DROP BATTER BY SPOONFULS ON TOP OF RHUBARB AND BAKE 35-40 MINUTES. SERVE WARM WITH ICE CREAM OR WHIPPED CREAM. SERVES 6.

PECAN SHORTBREAD SQUARES

CRUST

1 CUP BUTTER	250 mL
⅓ CUP FIRMLY PACKED BROWN SUGAR	75 mL
1 EGG	
1 TSP. LEMON JUICE	5 mL
3 CUPS FLOUR	750 mL
2 CUPS CHOPPED PECANS	500 mL

FILLING

¾ CUP BUTTER	175 mL
½ CUP HONEY	125 mL
¾ CUP BROWN SUGAR	175 mL
3 TBSP. CREAM	45 mL

TO MAKE CRUST: PREHEAT OVEN TO 350°F. THOROUGHLY MIX BUTTER, SUGAR, EGG, LEMON JUICE AND FLOUR AND PRESS INTO A 10" X 15" EDGED COOKIE SHEET. PRICK WITH A FORK AND BAKE FOR 20 MINUTES. SPREAD PECANS OVER CRUST.

TO MAKE FILLING: IN A HEAVY PAN, MELT BUTTER AND HONEY. ADD BROWN SUGAR AND BRING TO A BOIL, WHISKING CONTINUOUSLY, UNTIL DARK BROWN, 5-7 MINUTES. REMOVE FROM HEAT AND ADD CREAM IMMEDIATELY. MIX AND POUR OVER PECANS. RETURN TO OVEN FOR 20 MINUTES. COOL BEFORE CUTTING.

A GREAT ACTOR CAN BRING TEARS TO YOUR EYES. BUT THEN, SO CAN AN AUTO MECHANIC.

CHOCOLATE CARAMEL PECAN CHEESECAKE

YOU'LL WANT HELP REMOVING THE WRAPPERS FROM THE CARAMELS . . . SO GET THE KIDS TO DO IT (AND COUNT)!!

2 CUPS VANILLA WAFER CRUMBS	500 mL
1/3 CUP MARGARINE, MELTED	75 mL
14 OZ. PKG. KRAFT CARAMELS	400 g
6 OZ. CAN EVAPORATED MILK	170 mL
1 CUP CHOPPED PECANS, TOASTED	250 mL
2 - 8 OZ. PKGS. CREAM CHEESE, SOFTENED	500 g
1/2 CUP SUGAR	125 mL
1 TSP. VANILLA	5 mL
2 EGGS	
1/2 CUP SEMI-SWEET CHOCOLATE CHIPS, MELTED	125 mL

PREHEAT OVEN TO 350°F. COMBINE CRUMBS AND MARGARINE. PRESS INTO BOTTOM OF A 9" SPRINGFORM PAN AND BAKE FOR 10 MINUTES. IN A HEAVY SAUCEPAN, MELT CARAMELS WITH MILK OVER LOW HEAT, STIRRING OFTEN UNTIL SMOOTH. POUR OVER CRUST AND TOP WITH CHOPPED PECANS. COMBINE CHEESE, SUGAR AND VANILLA AND BEAT ON MEDIUM SPEED UNTIL WELL-BLENDED. ADD EGGS, ONE AT A TIME, MIXING WELL AFTER EACH ADDITION. BLEND IN MELTED CHOCOLATE AND POUR OVER PECANS. BAKE FOR 40 MINUTES. COOL AND LOOSEN CAKE FROM RIM OF PAN. CHILL. REMEMBER - CALORIES DON'T COUNT IF YOU EAT CHEESECAKE STANDING UP! SERVES 10-12 (SITTING DOWN OR STANDING UP!!)

GRANDMA'S CHRISTMAS PUDDING WITH GOLDEN SAUCE

1 LB. GROUND SUET	500 g
1 CUP BROWN SUGAR	250 mL
4 EGGS, WELL-BEATEN	
1 LB. CURRANTS	500 g
1 LB. DARK RAISINS	500 g
1 LB. SULTANA RAISINS	500 g
½ LB. MIXED PEEL	250 g
1 CUP PEELED & GRATED CARROTS	250 mL
1 CUP PEELED & GRATED POTATOES	250 mL
2 APPLES, PEELED & GRATED	
2 CUPS FLOUR	500 mL
1 LEMON, JUICE & RIND	
2 CUPS BREAD CRUMBS	500 mL
1 TSP. BAKING SODA	5 mL
2 TSP. CINNAMON	10 mL
½ TSP. EACH, ALLSPICE, CLOVES, SALT	2 mL
1 TBSP. MOLASSES	15 mL

IN A LARGE BOWL OR LARGE ROASTING PAN BLEND SUET AND SUGAR TOGETHER. ADD EGGS. MIX CURRANTS, RAISINS, PEEL, CARROTS, POTATOES AND APPLES WITH THE FLOUR TO COAT. SPRINKLE WITH LEMON JUICE AND RIND. ADD REMAINING INGREDIENTS AND MIX WELL. FILL STERILIZED PINT JARS (OR GREASED COVERED MOLDS) ⅔ FULL WITH PUDDING MIXTURE. STEAM FOR 3 HOURS. MAKES 13 PINTS. WHEN READY TO SERVE, STEAM FOR ½ HOUR OR HEAT IN MICROWAVE.

GRANDMA'S CHRISTMAS PUDDING WITH GOLDEN SAUCE

THIS RECIPE CONTINUED FROM PAGE 208.

TO STEAM: PLACE CONTAINERS ON A TRIVET OR RACK IN A HEAVY KETTLE OVER ONE INCH OF BOILING WATER. COVER KETTLE. USE HIGH HEAT TO BEGIN WITH, THEN AS STEAM BEGINS TO ESCAPE, REDUCE HEAT TO LOW FOR REMAINING COOKING TIME. CHECK WATER LEVEL PERIODICALLY AND ADD AS NECESSARY.

GOLDEN SAUCE

ALSO, A DANDY ADDITION TO ICE CREAM!

1 CUP BUTTER	250 mL
2 CUPS ICING SUGAR	500 mL
4 TBSP. CREAM	60 mL
2 EGGS, BEATEN	
PINCH OF SALT	
1 TBSP. VANILLA OR WHITE RUM	15 mL

COOK ALL INGREDIENTS OVER HOT WATER IN DOUBLE BOILER. BEAT OCCASIONALLY UNTIL THICK AND CREAMY. MAKES ABOUT 2 CUPS.

NOBODY'S HOME BUT THE FIRE - AND IT'S OUT!

BRUNCH 'N' LUNCH

BEST BUFFETS

BEST BUFFETS CONTINUED

APPETIZERS CONTINUED

CHICKEN, SZECHUAN SESAME WINGS	40
CHINESE PORK	39
EMPANADAS	32
GARLIC, BAKED STARTER	44
PASADENA PINWHEELS	38
PEPPER JELLY TURNOVERS	42
PESTO CHEESE BUNDLES	45
PETITE PASTIES	48
PIZZA, STACKED	43
SALSA, PICANTE	37
SPINACH BITES	41

SOUPS

BEAN, BEST OF BRIDGE	73
CARROT	70
CHEDDAR CORN CHOWDER	69
MELON, TWO-TONE	65
MINESTRONE, TUSCAN	72
PUMPKIN	71
RED PEPPER	68
STRAWBERRY, COLD	66
TOMATO, CREAM OF	67

SALADS

BROCCOLI MANDARIN	57
CHICKEN & ASPARAGUS	61
CRAB 'N' PASTA WITH GINGER DRESSING	64
DOUBLE GREEN	52
DRESSING	
- ORANGE SHERRY	55
- YOGURT CURRY	52
EGGNOG, MOLD	49

SALADS CONTINUED

LAYERED MOZZARELLA & TOMATO	63
MARINATED CHINESE NOODLES & VEGETABLES	62
PAPAYA AVOCADO	51
PEAR & WALNUT	50
SPINACH	
- MELON	56
- STRAWBERRY	55
SUNSHINE	60
WARM VINAIGRETTE	59
YUCATÁN SALAD	58

VEGETABLES

BEANS	
- GREEN GUIDO	90
- GREEN VINAIGRETTE	89
BRUSSELS SPROUTS, SAUSY	88
CARROTS	
- ARTICHOKE HEARTS	83
- PATCH	84
CELERY SAUTÉ	75
CHILI, BARBER'S BEST	76
MUSHROOMS AU GRATIN	87
PEPPERS	
- PERFECT	85
- JULIENNE	128
POTATOES	
- CRISPY OVEN-BAKED	78
- DRESSED UP SPUDS	79
- GARLIC HERBED	77
- OVEN-BAKED FRIES	79
- ROASTED NEW WITH HERBS	77
- SWISS	78
"RATATOOEE!"	74

VEGETABLES CONTINUED

RICE
- LEMON   80
- RISOTTO   82

SQUASH, SPICY SPAGHETTI   86
TOMATOES, FRIED GREEN   91

BEEF

BURGER, CAESAR   102
CHATEAUBRIAND WITH   100
    COGNAC SAUCE
CORNED BEEF & VEGGIES   98
FAJITAS, TEX-MEX   106
MEATLOAF, MAJOR GREY'S   101
OSSO BUCO MILANESE   108
SHORT RIBS, GRILLED   107
    KOREAN
SLOPPY JOE POTATOES   105
SZECHUAN BEEF WITH   110
    BROCCOLI
VEAL 'N' VERMOUTH   99

CHICKEN

BREASTS WITH ASPARAGUS   120
BURRITOS   114
CHILI, SOUTHWESTERN   116
FAJITAS, TEX-MEX   106
HONEY-MUSTARD   113
KABOBS, NO-BRAINER   141
LIME GRILLED   119
MAPLE ORANGE   118
ORANGE-ROSEMARY   111
OVEN-FRIED   117
PHEASANT MADEIRA   123
STICKEY BAKED   115

LAMB & PORK

LAMB
- CURRY   136
- RACK, MUSTARD COATING   137

PORK
- CROWN ROAST WITH   142
    APPLE RAISIN STUFFING
- KABOBS, NO-BRAINER   141
- LOIN ROAST   135
- MEDALLIONS   138

FISH & SEAFOOD

CIOPPINO   129
CRUNCHY OVEN-BAKED   134
HALIBUT
- GRILLED & PEPPERS   128
    JULIENNE
- ORANGE-GINGER   127

ORANGE ROUGHIE DIJONNAISE   126
SALMON, WILD WEST   125
SCALLOPS PAPRIKA   131
SHRIMP
- SCALLOP SUPREME   130
- STIR-FRY   132
- SZECHUAN   133

SNAPPER, BAKED ITALIANO   124

PASTA

ARTICHOKE SAUCE   143
CREAMY MUSHROOM   150
FETTUCCINI FLORENTINE   154
LASAGNA, PESTO   146
NOODLES, SINGAPORE FRIED   112
ORZO WITH PARMESAN   81
    & BASIL
PEPPERS, WITH PASTA   149
PEROGY, QUICK CASSEROLE   153
PIE, PASTA   148
ROTINI, SHRIMP IN CURRY   151
    GARLIC CREAM
SPAGHETTINI, WITH CHICKEN   152
TORTELLINI, RED & WHITE   144

"BADDIES" BUT GOODIES

CANDIES

CHOCOLATE TRUFFLES, GRAND MARNIER	165
PEPPERMINT BRITTLE	164

COOKIES

BISCOTTI	161
CHOCOLATE-CHOCOLATE CHIP	156
CHOCOLATE TRUFFLE	163
FRESH APPLE	158
GRANOLA, GRANDMA HUDSON'S	155
MACADAMIA CHOCOLATE	157
MACAROONS	164
ORANGE CHOCOLATE CHIP	159
SHORTBREAD, NANNY'S REAL SCOTTISH	160
SNICKERDOODLES	162

SQUARES

CHOCOLATE CARAMEL	177
CHOCOLATE PECAN BARS	178
CRANBERRY	176
PECAN SHORTBREAD	206
PUFFED WHEAT	179
RASPBERRY WALNUT LINZER	175

CAKES

APPLE	
- FRESH	170
- SOUR CREAM	167
MY LATEST FAVORITE	166
PECAN HOLIDAY	204
PLUM RUM	168

PIES

CHEDDAR APPLE TART	171
CHOCOLATE BRITTLE	182
RHUBARB-STRAWBERRY CRUMBLE	183
PEANUT BUTTER, FROZEN	184

DESSERTS

ACES	186
BLUEBERRY	
- BONANZA	200
- BUCKLE	198
CHANTILLY L'ORANGE	187
CHEESECAKE, CHOCOLATE CARAMEL PECAN	207
CHERRY-FILLED ANGEL	169
LEMON, FROZEN PUFF	185
MOUSSE, WHITE CHOCOLATE WITH RASPBERRY SAUCE	196
PUDDINGS	
- CAJUN BREAD WITH RUM SAUCE	190
- GRANDMA'S CHRISTMAS	208
- JAKE'S RICE	195
- UPSIDE-DOWN CHOCOLATE FUDGE	189
RHUBARB COBBLER	205
SHERBET, FRESH STRAWBERRY	199
TARTS	
- FRESH BERRY	202
- RASPBERRY PECAN WITH SOUR CREAM GLAZE	180

FAT-REDUCED RECIPES ARE INDICATED BY AN ASTERISK

B	-	BEST OF BRIDGE
E	-	ENJOY!
W	-	WINNERS
G	-	GRAND SLAM
A	-	ACES
T	-	THAT'S TRUMP

CURRIED CHUTNEY SPREAD	43	T
CURRIED SCALLOPS	44	E
CURRIED SEAFOOD COCKTAIL PUFFS	43	E
CURRY DIP FOR VEGETABLES	45	E
DILLED OYSTER CRACKERS	56	G
EMPANADAS	32	A
FLATBREAD, SEASONED	30	A
GUACAMOLE CHERRY TOMATO HALVES	37	W
HAM & CHEESE BALL	49	E
HAM & CHEESE PUFFS	64	G
JALAPEÑO PEPPER JELLY	55	W
JELLY BALLS	44	W
*JEZEBEL	43	T
LOBSTER DIP	48	E
MUSHROOM		
- HOT TURNOVERS	47	W
- SPINACH-STUFFED	52	W
- STUFFED CAPS	63	B
MUSSEL CREOLE	54	G
NACHOS, SUPER	48	W
NUTS & BOLTS	45	G
OYSTERS		
- CADILLAC	38	W
- SMOKED SPREAD	47	G
PASADENA PINWHEELS	38	A
PÂTÉ		
- COUNTRY	70	B
- JOHNNY'S MOMMY'S	47	E
- LIVER	69	B
- SALMON	53	G
- STILTON	37	T
PEACHY CHEESE DIP	34	A
PEPPER JELLY TURNOVERS	42	A
PEPPER RELISH	56	W
PESTO CHEESE BUNDLES	45	A
PETITE PASTIES	48	A
PICANTE SALSA	37	A
PIZZA, STACKED	43	A
PURK'S POO-POOS	53	E
QUESADILLAS		
- EL GRANDO CHICKEN	29	T

- BRIE AND PAPAYA	34	T
- CHEESE	46	A
QUICHE LORRAINE TARTS	68	B
RAILROAD DIP	52	W
RAREBIT-IN-A-HOLE	46	G
RUMAKI	51	E
SALMON		
- SMOKED	53	E
- SMOKED SUPERB	50	W
SEAFOOD		
- HOT DIP	73	B
- WINE	62	G
SHRIMP		
- CRUNCHY	49	E
- DIP	54	E
- MOLDED DIP	37	T
- PICKLED	74	B
SOURDOUGH, "GREY CUP"	31	T
SPANAKOPITA	58	G
SPINACH		
- BITES	41	A
- SPRINGTIME DIP	49	W
SWISS BACON PLEASERS	38	T
TAPENADE	42	T
*TZATZIKI	41	T
WONTON CRISPIES	39	T
ZUCCHINI SQUARES	38	T

BEEF

BONES	120	E
CORNED BEEF & VEGGIES	98	A
GROUND BEEF		
- BEAN STUFF	96	B
- BURGER, CAESAR	102	A
- BURRITOS	113	G
- CABBAGE ROLL CASSEROLE	114	G
- CABBAGE ROLLS	96	W
- CASSEROLE FOR A COLD NIGHT	157	T
- CHINESE	113	B
- ENCHILADAS	126	E

BEEF CONTINUED

GROUND BEEF CONTINUED
- FANDANGO   137 E
- GOULASH   131 E
- MEXICAN LASAGNE   156 T
- *PIE, SKILLET CHILI   154 T
- SATURDAY NIGHT   103 B
- SLOPPY JOE POTATOES   105 A
- TACO PIE   115 G
- TOURTIÈRE   88 B
- TOURTIÈRE   152 T

MEATBALLS
- JELLY BALLS   44 W
- ORIENTAL   94 B
- STROGANOFF   140 E

MEAT LOAF
- FAMILY FAVORITE   107 W
- MAJOR GREY'S   101 A

LIVER STIR-FRY   119 G

RIBS
- SHORT, IN BEER   151 E
- GRILLED KOREAN   107 A

ROASTS
- ENGLISH SPICED   150 E
- UNATTENDED   123 G

STEAK
- BAKED   100 B
- BEEF-ON-A-STICK   103 W
- BEEF & BURGUNDY   112 E
- BULGOGI   150 T
- CHATEAUBRIAND   100 A
   WITH COGNAC
- CHINESE   97 B
- EXTRAORDINAIRE   118 G
   WITH SAUCE DIANNE
- FAJITAS   106 A
- *FLANK, GINGER GARLIC   149 T
- FLANK, SUPER   104 W
- GINGER FRIED   120 G
- KABOBS, MUSHROOM   119 W
- *MEXICAN ROUNDUP   151 T
- SAUERBRATEN   111 W
- STROGANOFF GINGER'S   136 E
- SZECHUAN WITH   110 A
   BROCCOLI

BEEF CONTINUED

- TENDERLOIN WITH   148 T
   PEPPERCORN SAUCE
STEWING BEEF
- STONED   154 E
- STROGANOFF   116 G
VEAL
- MUSHROOMS   117 W
- 'N' VERMOUTH   99 A
- OSSO BUCO MILANESE   108 A
- SCALLOPINI   142 E
- *WITH ARTICHOKES   147 T

BEVERAGES

A REAL SMOOTHIE   44 G
BREAKFAST, BLENDER   12 E
*BLENDER BREAKFAST   6 T
BRANDY
- COFFEE FREEZE   14 E
- MINT CREAM   60 B
EGGNOG SUPREME   59 B
FALLEN ANGELS   27 T
FUZZY NAVELS   43 G
GLOGG   42 G
HELLO SUNSHINE!   14 E
LEMONADE
- BLENDER   58 B
- CONCENTRATE   60 B
MARGUARITAS   15 W
MID-SUMMER MADNESS   19 W
MONGOLIAN DINGBATS   11 E
MORNING FLIP, GERRY'S   11 E
ORANGE JULIUS   15 W
PUNCH
- GRADUATION   14 W
- TERRY'S   19 W
- WINTER   13 E
RUM
- BUTTERED, HOT   43 G
- CANADIENNE, HOT   10 E
- DAIQUIRI   10 E
- PEACH FROSTY   27 T
SKIP AND GO NAKED!   12 E

BEVERAGES CONTINUED

TEA
- BLUEBERRY — 13 E
- LONG ISLAND ICED — 44 G
- SPICED — 58 B

SANGRIA — 16 W

BREADS

*BAGUETTE, SUE'S X TWO — 23 T

BANANA
- BEST EVER — 21 G
- BLUEBERRY — 20 G
- GOING — 24 W

BISCUITS
- BUTTERMILK — 21 W
- FLAKY FREEZER — 28 A
- SAVORY CHEDDAR — 26 T

BLUEBERRY COFFEE CAKE — 18 E

BREAD
- APRICOT, L'IL RED'S — 26 E
- BROWN, STEAMED — 31 W
- CHEDDAR BEER — 25 A
- COFFEE CAN — 17 E
- COUNTRY CORN — 29 W
- FOCACCIA, OLIVE, ONION & ROSEMARY — 24 T
- FRENCH, DRESSED UP — 32 G
- GARLIC, PARMESAN — 16 B
- GINGER — 19 E
- HERB — 16 B
- JIFFY ORANGE — 15 B
- MAPLE SYRUP GRAHAM — 30 W
- MOLASSES BROWN — 23 G
- NAAN — 32 W
- OATMEAL — 20 W
- ORANGE HONEY — 16 E
- SEASONED FLAT — 30 A
- STRAWBERRY — 22 G
- TOMATO SAVORY — 24 A

BUNS
- CHEESY — 32 G
- CINNAMON — 29 A
- IRISH PAN — 14 B
- SOUR CREAM GINGER — 22 W

BREADS CONTINUED

CRESCENTS, LEMON CREAM — 27 A
FERGOSA — 24 E
JALAPEÑO CORN STICKS — 25 W

LOAVES
- CHRISTMAS, CARROT — 12 B
- CINNAMON — 26 A
- LEMON — 22 E
- PINEAPPLE — 23 W
- PUMPKIN — 20 E
- ZUCCHINI — 25 E

MELBA HERB TOASTS — 25 T
NEW ORLEANS STRIPS — 11 B
PITA TOASTS — 31 G
SCONES, CRANBERRY — 15 T
SPICY BREAD STICKS — 30 W
TEA SCONES — 34 G
TEXAS TOAST — 25 T
WELSH CAKES — 33 G

BRUNCHES

ASPARAGUS PUFF — 136 W
BACON, CAMPTOWN — 9 A
BREAKFAST FRUIT KABOBS — 7 A

CASSEROLES
- SEAFOOD — 19 G
- STAMPEDE — 10 A
- WEEKENDER SPECIAL — 12 W

CHEESE SOUFFLÉ — 36 E
CHICKEN SCRAMBLE — 32 E
CHRISTMAS WIFE SAVER — 33 E
CLAFOUTI, PEACH AND BLUEBERRY — 7 T

EGGS
- BAKED — 35 E
- FLORENTINE — 13 G
- OLÉ — 12 G
- OMELETTE, BRIE, FRESH HERB & TOMATO — 12 T
- RANCHERO — 31 E
- SCOTTY'S NEST EGGS — 11 T
- SUNDAY HAM — 7 W

BRUNCHES CONTINUED

FRENCH TOAST
- MIDNIGHT .... 7 G
- RAPHAEL .... 14 A

LUNCHEON SOUFFLÉ ROLL ... 88 W

MEDITERRANEAN PIE .... 6 A

MUFFULETTA .... 13 T

QUICHE
- CRABMEAT .... 38 B
- CRUSTLESS .... 13 W
- LORRAINE .... 15 G
- SHRIMP & CRAB .... 40 B
- SWISS APPLE .... 8 G
- TOMATO, CHEESE & ..... 8 T
   HERB TART

SAUSAGE
- BASHAW BISTRO RING ... 13 A
- 'N' JOHNNY CAKE ...... 14 G
- PIE .... 10 G
- SENSATIONAL ROLL ..... 8 W
- WEEKEND SPOUSE SAVER . 10 T

STRATA
- CHEESE & TOMATO ...... 10 W
- MEXICAN .... 8 A

*SWISS BREAKFAST MUESLI . 6 T

CAKES

APPLE
- DUTCH .... 196 E
- FRESH .... 170 A
- SOUR CREAM .... 167 A

APPLESAUCE SPICE .... 204 B

CHOCOLATE
- CHIFFON .... 186 W
- DARK .... 191 G
- GRAND .... 174 E
- MOUSSE .... 184 G
- POUNDCAKE .... 177 E
- SUPER .... 206 B
- ZUCCHINI .... 190 W

CHRISTMAS
- CHERRY .... 165 E
- LIGHT .... 202 B

CAKES CONTINUED

COFFEE CAKES
- BLUEBERRY .... 18 E
- CHRISTMAS .... 23 E
- COCONUT WHIP .... 191 W
- *CRANAPPLE .... 14 T
- PECAN HOLIDAY .... 204 A
- SOUR CREAM .... 27 E

CRATER .... 194 W

CUPCAKES, BLACK BOTTOM .. 185 W

CUPCAKES, CHEESECAKE .... 188 E

FRUIT COCKTAIL .... 160 B

KARROT'S .... 162 E

LAZY DAISY .... 207 B

MOCHA WHIPPED CREAM ..... 196 G

MY LATEST FAVORITE ...... 166 A

ORANGE, ARMENIAN .... 172 E

PLUM RUM .... 168 A

POPPY SEED .... 174 W

POPPY SEED CHIFFON ...... 192 G

PRUNE .... 203 B

RHUBARB .... 163 E

WAR .... 164 E

CONFECTIONS

ALMONDS
- CANDIED .... 149 B
- ROCA .... 166 W
- SOYA .... 55 E

BOURBON BALLS .... 168 W

CASHEWS OR PECANS
- SPICED .... 57 E
- CHEWY TOFFEE .... 173 T
- CRISPIX MIX .... 175 T

CHOCOLATE
- FUDGE .... 192 B
- NUTCHOS .... 174 T
- PEANUT BUTTER BALLS .. 171 G
- TIGER BUTTER .... 171 T
- TRUFFLES .... 165 A
- TURTLES .... 172 T

CRACKER JACK .... 176 T

CRAZY CRUNCH .... 58 E

E-Z POPCORN BALLS .... 174 T

CONFECTIONS CONT'D

NUTS AND BOLTS	45	G
NUTS, NOVEL	56	E
PEANUT BRITTLE, MICROWAVE	162	G
PEPPERMINT BRITTLE	164	A
TRAIL MIX, TOM'S	57	E
WALNUTS, CARAMELLED	55	E
XMAS TOFFEE	173	T

COOKIES

ALMOND FLORENTINES	167	W
APPLE, FRESH	158	A
B.L.'S	163	G
BISCOTTI	161	A
BOURBON BALLS	168	W
BROWN BAGGER'S SPECIAL	160	W
CHEWY KIDS	158	W
CHOCOLATE		
- CHIP	167	E
- CHIP, SLAB	161	W
- CHOCOLATE CHIP	156	A
- *ESPRESSO COOKIES	168	T
- FATAL ATTRACTIONS	168	G
- FUDGE BALLS	150	B
- MACADAMIA	157	A
- ORANGE, CHIP	159	A
- PEANUT CHEWY BARS	170	W
- SNOWBALLS	148	B
- SKOR BAR	167	T
- TRUFFLE	163	A
CINNAMON, GLAZED BARS	163	W
CITRUS CRISPS	170	T
COCONUT BARS	159	W
COOKIE OF THE MONTH	164	T
DATE-FILLED COOKIES	165	T
DIAMONDS	170	E
FORGOTTEN COOKIES	139	B
GINGER SNAPS	169	G
GRANOLA	155	A
HERMITS	169	E
MACAROONS	164	A
MERINGUE, AFTER	157	W
MISSION CRY BABIES	166	E
MONA'S MOTHER'S	144	B

COOKIES CONTINUED

ONE CUP OF EVERYTHING	166	T
PEANUT BUTTER	165	G
PECAN CRISPS	166	G
PECAN MACAROONS	140	B
PEPPERNUTS	164	W
POPPY SEED	167	G
PRALINES	143	B
RAISIN, SOFT	147	B
SCOTCH SQUARES	165	W
SHORTBREAD	145	B
- BROWN SUGAR	171	T
- CHEESE	146	B
- FRUIT & NUT	168	E
- JEWISH	145	B
- NANNY'S REAL	160	A
- WHIPPED	146	B
SNICKERDOODLES	162	A
SNOWBALLS	148	B
SWEDISH PASTRY	143	B
VANILAS KIFLEI	169	T
WAFER PUFFS	162	W
ZUCCHINI	164	G

CRUSTS & PASTRY

CHOCOLATE WAFER	209	B
GRAHAM CRACKER	209	B
PASTRY, FAIL-PROOF	200	W
PECAN OR WALNUT	205	G
PUFF PASTRY SHELLS	210	B

DESSERTS

A "GRAND CAKE"	174	E
ANGEL FOOD FLAN	154	B
ANGEL MOCHA TORTE	152	B
APPLE BETTY		
- SOCIAL	208	B
- SPIKED	171	W
APPLE		
- EASIER THAN APPLE PIE	188	T
- KUCHEN	201	W
- *PECAN PHYLLO CRISPS	190	T
- ROLL	156	B

APRICOT SMOOCH	189	E
BANANA GINGER LOAF	182	W
BERRY TART, FRESH	202	A
BLUEBERRY		
- BONANZA	200	A
- BUCKLE	198	A
- DELIGHT	184	B
BRANDY SNAPS	158	B
BUTTER BRICKLE	169	B
CARDINAL'S LIME	178	E
CHANTILLY L'ORANGE	187	A
CHEESECAKE	151	B
- CHOCOLATE CARAMEL	207	A
- CUPCAKES	188	E
- *RASPBERRY CREAM WITH BLUEBERRY COULIS	198	T
- PUMPKIN	179	G
CHERRIES JUBILEE	168	B
CHERRY ANGEL FOOD	169	A
CHERRY BERRIES	192	W
CHOCOLATE		
- ACES	186	A
- CHEESE TORTE	182	E
- CHIFFON	186	W
- MOCHA MOUSSE	181	E
- *MOCHA MOUSSE	205	T
- *MOCHA PAVLOVA	204	T
- MOCHA TORTE	166	B
- MOCHA TORTE	199	E
- POTS DE CRÈME	193	E
- RASPBERRY TORTE	177	W
- ROLL	190	E
- SABAYON	189	G
- TORTE ROYALE	180	B
- UPSIDE-DOWN CAKE	171	E
- UPSIDE-DOWN FUDGE PUDDING	189	A
- WHITE CHOCOLATE MOUSSE, RASPBERRY	196	A
CRÈME CARAMEL	188	G
CRÈME DE MENTHE	164	B
DACQUOISE CAFÉ	202	T
DANISH RUM SOUFFLÉ	194	E

DATE TORTE	195	E
FRUIT COCKTAIL CAKE	160	B
*FRUIT COCKTAIL, MARGUARITA	207	T
FRUIT POOF	180	W
GRAND MARNIER CRÈME	193	W
GRAND SLAM FINALE	187	G
GRASSHOPPER CAKE	186	E
HAZELNUT TORTE	194	G
LEMON		
- BERRY CAKE	182	B
- FROZEN MOUSSE & RASPBERRY SAUCE	196	W
- FROZEN PUFF	185	A
- ICE BOX PUDDING	170	B
- PUDDING	192	E
- SORBET	190	G
- STRAWBERRY ANGEL TARTS	174	B
MARSHMALLOW COFFEE	189	B
MELON & RUM SAUCE	198	E
MIZ VICKY'S TEMPTATION	189	T
ORANGE ANGEL TORTE	200	T
PAVLOVA	203	W
PEACH		
- BRANDIED	183	B
- EASY TORTE	195	W
- FLAMBÉ	163	B
- FROSTY	180	G
- *VANILLA PEACH SHERBET	208	T
PEPPERMINT		
- CANDY	188	B
- ICE CREAM	185	B
PINEAPPLE SLICE	162	B
PUDDINGS		
- CAJUN BREAD	190	A
- *ENGLISH BERRY	196	T
- GRANDMA'S CHRISTMAS	208	A
- JAKE'S RICE	195	A
- LEMON	192	E
- MARGAREE CRANBERRY	194	T
- *RHUBARB BREAD	193	T

DESSERTS CONTINUED

- UPSIDE-DOWN CHOCOLATE FUDGE	189	A
QUICK FROZEN RASPBERRY	173	B
- *CREAM WITH BLUEBERRY COULIS	198	T
- PECAN TART & SOUR CREAM GLAZE	180	A
RHUBARB		
- COBBLER	205	A
- CREAM	188	W
- CRISP WITH BOURBON SAUCE	182	G
- *RHUBARB BREAD PUDDING	193	T
- RHUBARB DELIGHT	181	G
RUM CAKE	153	B
SABAYON, STELLA	193	G
STRAWBERRY		
- ANGEL FOOD CAKE	187	B
- CRÊPES	178	B
- FRESH DELIGHT	173	E
- LEMON ANGEL TARTS	174	B
- PUFF PANCAKE	172	B
- SHERBET, FRESH	199	A
TIA MARIA CAKE	200	E
TIRAMISU	186	G
TOFFEE MERINGUE	183	G
TRIFLE, ENGLISH	184	E
WHISKEY FLIP	206	T

FISH & SEAFOOD

ARCTIC CHAR, STUFFED	104	E
BAKED FISH MOZZARELLA	127	G
CIOPPINO	129	A
CRAB		
- CASSEROLE	41	B
- CASSEROLE, BAKED	42	B
- CRÊPES	34	B
- CURRIED, TETRAZZINI	110	B
- LUNCHEON SOUFFLÉ	88	W
- QUICHE	38	B
CRUNCHY OVEN-BAKED	134	A

FISH & SEAFOOD CONT'D

HALIBUT		
- CHOWDER	79	T
- GRILLED & PEPPERS JULIENNE	128	A
- ORANGE GINGER	127	A
- WINE POACHED	126	G
LOBSTER NEWBURG	84	B
MARINATED FISH FILLETS WITH BASIL BUTTER	128	G
MUSSELS & SCALLOPS IN CREAM	130	G
ORANGE ROUGHIE DIJONNAISE	126	A
*ORANGE ROUGHIE POLYNESIAN	138	T
OYSTER SCALLOP	106	E
SALMON		
- CHILLED SOUFFLÉ	108	E
- *POACHED WITH PIQUANT SAUCE	136	T
- POTLATCH	129	G
- STEAKS, BAR-B-QUED	105	E
- STEAKS, TERIYAKI	127	G
- STUFFING		
- RICE & OLIVE	106	E
- WILD WEST	125	A
SCALLOPS		
- COQUILLE DAVID	122	E
- IN WINE	85	B
SCALLOPS		
- PAPRIKA	131	A
- SHELLS, SEAFOOD	39	B
SCAMPI	102	E
SEAFOOD		
- CASSEROLE	19	G
- CREAMED	86	B
- CURRY	82	B
- KABOBS	131	G
SHELLFISH PUKÉ	148	E
SHRIMP		
- & CRAB QUICHE	40	B
- & RICE & ARTICHOKES	140	T
- & SCALLOP SUPREME	130	A

FISH & SEAFOOD CONT'D

SHRIMP CONTINUED
- IN FOIL — 112 B
- *ORANGE STIR-FRIED — 144 T
- PARTY — 111 B
- STIR-FRY — 132 A
- STROGANOFF — 80 B
- SZECHUAN — 133 A

SNAPPER
- BAKED ITALIANO — 124 A
- CREAMY DILLED — 124 G
- *PARMESAN — 139 T

SOLE
- BAKED ROULADE — 109 E
- O-MIO — 125 G
- YOU GOTTA HAVE — 102 E

*TUNA, LAYERED CASSEROLE — 143 T

FOWL

CHICKEN
- ALMOND — 110 E
- *AMARETTO — 122 T
- BALLS — 78 B
- BARBECUE, MARINADE — 139 E
- *BARE-NAKED — 121 T
- BRANDIED, SAMS — 100 W
- BREASTS, ASPARAGUS — 120 A
- BREASTS, STUFFED — 102 B
- *BREASTS, ZELDA — 125 T
- BURRITOS — 114 A
- CANTONESE — 133 E
- CASSEROLE — 81 B
  - ARTICHOKE — 87 W
  - ENCHILADA — 153 G
  - MANDALAY — 154 G
  - MEXICANA — 159 G
  - 'N' NOODLE — 121 E
  - POLYNESIAN — 79 B
  - *SZECHUAN — 130 T
  - THIGH — 132 T
  - WILD RICE — 152 E
  - WINE — 107 B
  - YUMMY — 86 W
- CATCH-A-TORY — 152 G
- CHILI, SOUTHWESTERN — 116 A

FOWL CONTINUED

- CLASSY — 85 W
- CRAB, STUFFED — 124 E
- CRÊPES — 34 B
- CRISPY SESAME — 146 G
- DIVINE, DIVAN — 138 E
- ENCHILADAS — 110 W
- FAJITAS, TEX MEX — 106 A
- FINGERS — 129 T
- FRIED RICE — 98 B
- *GRILLED LEMON HERB — 128 T
- HONEY MUSTARD — 113 A
- JAMBALAYA — 153 E
- KABOBS — 141 A
- LASAGNE — 114 W
- LEMON — 111 E
- LIME GRILLED — 119 A
- MAPLE-ORANGE — 118 A
- *MEDALLIONS — 126 T
- ORANGE ROSEMARY — 111 A
- OVEN-FRIED — 117 A
- PARMESAN — 149 G
- POT PIE — 155 G
- QUESADILLA, EL GRANDO — 29 T
- STICKY BAKED — 115 A
- SWEET 'N' SPICY CASHEW — 148 G
- TETRAZZINI — 92 W
- TORTILLA LASAGNE — 120 T
- WHIPLASH — 156 G
- WINGS
  - CURRIED — 109 B
  - JAPANESE — 106 B

CORNISH HENS — 150 G

DUCK
- BREAST EN CASSEROLE — 147 G
- ROAST, WITH ORANGE SAUCE — 146 E / 147 E

PHEASANT
- ALMOND ORANGE — 150 G
- CASSEROLE — 133 T
- MADEIRA — 123 A
- PIE — 134 T

FOWL CONTINUED

STUFFING
- TURKEY, TERRIFIC — 40 G

TURKEY CASSEROLE — 108 B

ICING & DESSERT SAUCES

DRESSING
- FRESH FRUIT — 206 G
- FRUIT DIP — 206 G
- POPPY SEED — 119 B

ICING
- FLUFFY — 160 E
- ISLA'S — 191 B
- LEMON, FLUFFY — 20 E
  CREAM TOPPING
- VANILLA, CREAMY — 191 B
  FROSTING

SAUCES
- *BLUEBERRY COULIS — 198 T
- CRÈME FRAÎCHE — 196 T
- DELUXE — 190 B
- FOAMY BUTTER — 191 E
- FUDGE — 191 E
- FUDGE, HOT — 173 W
- GOLDEN — 208 A
- LEMON — 185 T
- *MOCK CRÈME FRAÎCHE — 196 T
- RASPBERRY — 196 A
- RUM — 190 A
- *SINFULLY RICH FUDGE — 195 T

LAMB

CURRY — 136 A
LEG, RED CURRANT — 84 W
MARINATED, BARBECUED — 116 W
MOUSSAKA — 108 W
RACK, MUSTARD COATING — 137 A
SOUVLAKI — 158 T
STEW, GREEK — 159 T

MUFFINS

APPLE CINNAMON — 21 E
BACK-PACKING — 21 T
BANANA — 29 G

MUFFINS CONTINUED

BLUEBERRY, LEMON — 15 E
BRAN, A PAIL FULL — 20 A
CARROT & RAISIN — 27 G
CHEESE
- & BACON — 28 G
- CHEDDAR APPLE — 15 A
- CHEDDAR DILL — 27 W
- CREAM — 24 G
CRANBERRY — 16 A
*GUILT-REDUCED BRAN — 22 T
HEALTH NUT — 30 G
LUNCH BOX — 23 A
MINCEMEAT — 26 W
*MORNING GLORY — 20 T
OAT — 13 B
OAT BRAN — 21 A
ORANGE
- MANDARIN — 25 G
- SUNSHINE — 28 W
PIZZA — 22 A
PUMPKIN PECAN — 19 A
*RASPBERRY-FILLED — 19 T
  CINNAMON
RHUBARB, PHANTOM — 26 G
SCONES, CRANBERRY — 15 T
STRAWBERRY — 16 T

PASTA

BALSAMIC — 112 T
CANNELLONI — 114 E
CHICKEN, SPAGHETTINI — 152 A
CRAB & BASIL — 134 G
FETTUCCINE
- FLORENTINE — 154 A
- VERDE — 121 W
- LEMON — 107 T
- SAMBUCA & CRANBERRIES — 115 T
- *WITH ASPARAGUS & — 117 T
  SHRIMP
FRESH TOMATO & CHEESE — 111 T
LASAGNE — 104 B
- BROCCOLI — 145 G
- CHICKEN — 114 W

PASTA CONTINUED

LASAGNE CONTINUED
- CHICKEN TORTILLA   120 T
- HAM & MUSHROOM   136 G
- MEXICAN LASAGNE   156 T
- PESTO   146 A
- SEAFOOD   103 E
- SPINACH   143 G
- VEGETABLE   119 T
GORGONZOLA   108 T
LINGUINI
- CLAM SAUCE   122 W
- RED CLAM SAUCE   133 G
MACARONI, GOURMET   135 G
MANICOTTI   102 W
NOODLES, SINGAPORE   112 A
ORZO, PARMESAN & BASIL   81 A
PASTA POT   120 W
PENNE - SPICY   142 G
PEPPERS   149 A
PEROGY - CASSEROLE   153 A
PIE   148 A
PRIMAVERA   138 G
*PUTTANESCA   116 T
ROTINI, SHRIMP IN   151 A
  GARLIC CREAM
SAUCES
- ALFREDO   83 W
- *ALFREDO, ACCEPTABLE   109 T
- ARTICHOKE   143 A
- CREAMY MUSHROOM   150 A
- GAFFER'S   128 E
- ITALIAN SAUSAGE   132 G
- MINDLESS MEAT   117 E
- PESTO   127 W
*SHRIMP AND TOMATO   118 T
SPAGHETTI
- CARBONARA   144 G
- WITH EGGPLANT   114 B
SPINACH AND FETA   113 T
TORTELLINI
- RED & WHITE   144 A
- WITH THREE CHEESES   110 T
*VEGGIE, LIGHT   114 T

PIES

CHOCOLATE
- BRITTLE   182 A
- LINCOLN CENTRE   197 E
- MINT   157 B
- MOUSSE   189 W
- MUD   180 E
- PECAN   203 G
COFFEE ICE CREAM   161 B
CRANBERRY CUSTARD   186 T
FLAPPER   172 W
FUDGE, CUSTARD SAUCE   198 G
GRASSHOPPER   165 B
IRISH COFFEE CREAM   198 W
JALAPEÑO APPLE   187 T
LEMON, FRENCH   201 G
LIME PARFAIT   173 B
*MINCEMEAT TARTS   184 T
PALACE   200 G
PEACHES & CREAM   197 G
PEANUT BUTTER   184 A
PECAN   179 E
PUMPKIN
- CHIFFON   184 W
- PECAN   202 W
RHUBARB
- MERINGUE   204 G
- STRAWBERRY CRUMBLE   183 A
RUM CREAM   171 B
SHOO-FLY   187 W
TIN ROOF   202 G

PORK

CHINESE   87 B
CHOP SUEY   134 E
CHOP SUEY, NOODLE   112 W
CUTLETS, CAJUN PORK   163 T
DUMPLINGS   98 W
HAM
- APRICOTS   119 E
- BEER   82 W
- CASSEROLE   141 E
- JAMBALAYA   153 E
- LOAF   161 G

PORK CONTINUED

KABOBS, NO-BRAINER	141	A
MEDALLIONS	138	A
PEACHY	130	E
RIBS		
- DRY	99	B
- GREEK	117	G
- ORANGE SPUNKY	97	W
- SWEET & SOUR	144	E
- SWEET & SOUR CHILI	132	E
ROAST		
- BARBECUED	90	W
- CROWN, APPLE RAISIN STUFFING	142	A
- LOIN	135	A
- LOIN WITH APPLE	161	T
SATAY	129	E
STUFFING		
- APPLE RAISIN	142	A
- CRANBERRY	39	G
TENDERLOIN		
CASHEWS	94	W
STUFFED	162	T
WITH HONEY-GLAZED APPLES	160	T
TOMATO CANTONESE	160	G
TOURTIÈRE	88	B
TOURTIÈRE	152	T

PIZZA

CARAMELIZED ONION & CHÈVRE	99	T
FAST AND EASY CRUST	96	T
MARINATED SUN-DRIED TOMATOES	101	T
MEXICAN	102	T
ORIENTAL CHICKEN	104	T
PEAR AND CAMBOZOLA	97	T
PESTO	98	T
PRIMAVERA	100	T

SALADS

ARTICHOKE		
- MARINATED, MUSHROOM	68	W
- ZUCCHINI	60	W
AVOCADO, FRUIT	127	B
BEET, RUSSIAN	78	G
BROCCOLI, MANDARIN	57	A
CAESAR	121	B
CANLIS	61	E
CHICKEN		
- ASPARAGUS	61	A
- *BARBECUED THAI	46	T
- CAESAR	50	T
- CURRIED BOATS	50	B
- FIESTA TORTILLA	45	T
- FRUIT & LIME	88	G
- GRILLED & SPINACH	48	T
- KOREAN	64	W
- LAYERED	57	W
COLE SLAW		
- KILLER	76	G
- PICKLED	60	E
- PINEAPPLE	128	B
COMMITTEE	66	W
CUCUMBER, LEE HONG'S	64	E
CURRIED RICE	52	T
FOO YUNG, TOSSED	65	E
FRENCH POTATO	58	T
FRUIT		
- ARIZONA	86	G
- AVOCADO	127	B
- MANDARIN ORANGE	71	E
- MARINATED	89	G
- *'N' SPINACH	64	T
- PAPAYA AVOCADO	51	A
- PEAR & WALNUT	50	A
- SUNSHINE	60	A
- WALDORF	120	B
- YUCATÁN	58	A
GREEK	70	W
GREEN BEAN & ONION	59	T
LAYERED	69	E
MEXICAN CHEF	46	B

MOLDED
- CHICKEN ATLANTA   62 W
- CHICKEN GUMBO   56 B
- COTTAGE CHEESE   57 B
- CUCUMBER CREAM   62 E
- EGGNOG   49 A
- FRUIT COCKTAIL   55 B
- HORSERADISH   117 B
- LOBSTER MOUSSE   48 B
- PINK FROSTY   125 B
- *SALSA MOLD   65 T
- TOMATO ASPIC   52 B

MUSHROOM, HOT   59 W
ORIENTAL GARDEN TOSS   67 W
PASTA
- ASPARAGUS   84 G
- CHINESE NOODLES   62 A
- CRAB 'N' GINGER   64 A
- SALMON   82 G
- SHOW-OFF TORTELLINI   57 T
- VEGETABLE   73 W

PEACHTREE PLAZA   69 W
POTATO, FRENCH   58 T
ROASTED RED PEPPER   49 T
ROMAINE
- DOUBLE GREEN   52 A
- ORANGES & PECANS   80 G
*SANTA FE   60 T
SEAFOOD
- AVOCADO CRAB   44 B
- BUFFET   59 E
- GREEN GODDESS   63 E
- SENATE   45 B
- WITH TARRAGON
    MUSTARD DRESSING   55 T
SHRIMP
- BOATS   47 B
- LOUIS   66 E
- PAPAYA   81 G
- PICKLED CITRUS   56 T
- SALAD   49 B

SPINACH
- ARMENIAN   70 E
- DIFFERENT   79 G
- FRESH   116 B
- MELON   56 A
- *'N' FRUIT   64 T
- ROYALE   71 E
- SOUR CREAM   61 W
- STRAWBERRY   55 A
- WARM, APPLES & BRIE   62 T
- WILTED   117 B

STRAWBERRY, CHÉVRE   63 T
SUNOMONO PLATTER   67 E
SUPER   126 B
TOMATO
- MARINATED   118 B
- MOZZARELLA   63 A
VEGETABLE MARINATED   115 B
VINAIGRETTE, WARM   59 A
*WILD RICE   61 T
ZUCCHINI   77 G

SALAD DRESSINGS

*BALSAMIC POPPY SEED   65 T
*BALSAMIC VINAIGRETTE   66 T
BLUE CHEESE   87 G
FRESH FRUIT   83 G
ITALIAN   67 T
JALAPEÑO LIME   50 T
MAYO, DOCTORED   58 W
ORANGE SHERRY   55 A
PESTO   73 W
POPPY SEED   119 B
TARRAGON MUSTARD   55 T
THOUSAND ISLAND   85 G
YOGURT CURRY   52 A

SANDWICHES

ASPARAGUS	28	B
BRIDGE PIZZAS	23	B
COCKTAIL	26	B
CRAB		
- CHEESE BUNS	26	B
- CHEESE TOASTIES	21	B
- DEVILED EGG	21	B
GOURMET TOAST	19	B
GRILLED CHEESE		
- ITALIANO	31	B
- THE UTMOST	16	G
HAM		
- BUNS	32	B
- CHEESE TOWERS	25	B
- FILLED	20	B
- 'N' CHEESE PARTY	29	B
- OPEN FACE	34	B
- SPINACH BAGUETTE	11	A
- STUFFED LOAF	29	E
LOAF, RENE'S	30	B
MUFFELETTA	13	T
PÂTÉ EN BAGUETTE	12	A
REUBEN	27	B
SEAFOOD SALAD	23	B
SHRIMP		
- FAST ROLLS	22	B
- SANDWICHES	28	E
SUNDAY	30	E
TACOS	24	B
TOMATO CHEESIES	34	E
TUNA PIZZA BURGER	33	B

SAUCES & RELISHES

CHUTNEY	134	B
- CRANBERRY & RAISIN	96	A
- HOT PEPPER ORANGE	44	T
JALAPEÑO PEPPER JELLY	55	W
MARMALADE		
- CARROT	94	A
- CHRISTMAS	37	E
- GREEN TOMATO	38	G
MINCEMENT, GREEN TOMATO	97	A
MUSTARD		
- B.L.'S PICKLES	95	A
- HOT & SWEET	93	A

SAUCES CONTINUED

MUSTARD		
- MONK'S	130	W
- TARRAGON	131	W
- *SAUCE	94	T
RELISHES		
- CORN	37	G
- GREEN TOMATO	133	B
- PEPPER RELISH	56	W
- PICALILLI	35	G
- PLUM, BLUE	38	E
- RHUBARB	92	B
- ZUCCHINI	126	W
SALSAS		
- *KIWI SALSA	92	T
- *ORANGE PEPPER AND CORN	93	T
- SALSA	95	W
- PICANTE	37	A
SAUCES		
- B.B.Q.	95	T
- CHILI	132	B
- CRANBERRY BURGUNDY	136	B
- CRANBERRY GOURMET	38	G
- CUMBERLAND	129	W
- GUACAMOLE	37	W
- HOLLANDAISE, BLENDER	92	A
- GINGER SOY	135	B
- MUSTARD	101	B
- FOR HAM	136	B
- FOR STEAK	101	B
- PEANUT	36	G
- PESTO	127	W
- PLUM	125	W
- TERIYAKI	135	B
SEASONINGS		
- CREOLE	92	A
- FLOUR	41	G
- SALT, SUBSTITUTE	41	G
STUFFINGS		
- APPLE RAISIN	142	A
- CRANBERRY	39	G
- RICE & OLIVE	106	E
- TURKEY, TERRIFIC	40	G
WINE CORDIAL	125	W

SOUPS

AVGOLEMONO	67	G
AVOCADO	68	G
BEAN, BEST OF BRIDGE	73	A
*BEEF VEGETABLE STOCK	82	T
*BLACK BEAN, MEXICAN	76	T
*BORSCH, SPRING	74	T
BROCCOLI	74	W
CARROT	70	A
CAULIFLOWER, BLUE CHEESE	73	G
CHEDDAR CORN CHOWDER	69	A
*CHICKEN & MATZO BALLS	80	T
CLAM CHOWDER	75	E
CRAB BISQUE	76	E
CRAB & CORN CHOWDER	74	E
CREAM OF		
- CRAB	76	E
- CUCUMBER	77	E
- CURRY	75	W
- PARSLEY & BASIL	71	G
- SPINACH	72	G
- TOMATO	67	A
CUCUMBER, CREAM OF	77	E
CURRY, CREAM OF	75	W
EGG DROP	76	W
ELEPHANT	79	E
FISHERMAN'S CHOWDER	77	W
GAZPACHO	130	B
GARLIC	70	T
*HALIBUT, JUST FOR THE, CHOWDER	79	T
HAMBURGER	129	B
HERB, WITH SHRIMP	79	W
*LENTIL, QUICK	75	T
MELON		
- GINGERED	76	W
- TWO-TONE	65	A
MINESTRONE	73	E
- TUSCAN	72	A
MULLIGATAWNY	66	G
MUSHROOM	78	W
- & LEEK	75	G
ONION, FRENCH	81	W
OYSTER STEW	131	B

SOUPS CONTINUED

PARSLEY, CREAM OF	71	G
PEA, HABITANT	78	E
POTATO	74	G
POTATO & LEEK	73	T
PUMPKIN	71	A
*RASPBERRY	68	T
RED PEPPER	68	A
SPINACH, CREAM OF	72	G
STRAWBERRY, COLD	66	A
TOMATO, CREAM OF	67	A
*TOMATO, FRESH, PESTO	69	T
TOMATO BISQUE, FRESH	80	W
*TORTELINI, HEARTY	78	T
TURKEY	72	E
*WAR WONTON	81	T
*ZUPPA DU JOUR	77	T

SQUARES

APPLE BROWNIES	183	T
BROWNIES	205	B
BROWNIES, FUDGE	161	E
BUTTER TART SLICE	172	G
CARAMEL BARS	157	E
CARAMEL NUT BROWNIES	182	T
CHEESE	195	B
CHOCOLATE		
- CARAMEL	177	A
- CRUNCH BARS	177	T
- PECAN	178	A
- ROCKY MOUNTAIN	173	G
- UNTURTLE BAR	179	T
- VERNA'S	201	B
CRANBERRY	176	A
DREAM SLICE	194	B
FUDGE SCOTCH	192	B
EAT MORE..MORE...MORE...	181	T
GEORGE (NANAIMO)	198	B
JOSHUA'S MOM'S SKATING BARS	180	T
LEMON BARS	158	E
MAGIC COOKIE BARS	196	B
MATRIMONIAL	170	G
MEXICAN WEDDING CAKE	197	B

SQUARES CONTINUED

MRS. LARSON'S BARS	159	E
PEANUT BUTTER		
- BROWNIES	174	G
- CRUNCHIES	197	B
- SLICE	196	B
PECAN SHORTBREAD	206	A
PEPPERMINT BARS	186	B
PUFFED WHEAT	179	A
RASPBERRY	193	B
RASPBERRY WALNUT	175	A
RICE KIRSPIE SQUARES	178	T
TOFFEE KRISPS	178	T

TARTS

BUTTER	200	B
CHEDDAR APPLE	171	A
*MINCEMEAT	184	T
PECAN CUPS	177	G
SHORTBREAD	199	B
TART FILLINGS		
- CHEESE & FRUIT	178	G
- LEMON BUTTER	189	B
- LEMON CHEESE	199	B
- GREEN TOMATO MINCEMEAT	97	A

VEGETABLES

ASPARAGUS		
- BAKED	91	G
- NOODLE BAKE	92	G
- PUFF	136	W
BEANS		
- BAKED	148	W
- CALICO POT	94	G
- GREEN, CASSEROLE	89	E
- GREEN, GUIDO	90	A
- GREEN, MANDARIN	149	W
- GREEN, SUDDEN VALLEY	145	W
- GREEN, VINAIGRETTE	89	A
- SPEEDY, BAKED	95	G

VEGETABLES CONTINUED

BROCCOLI		
- CASSEROLE	100	E
- EASTER	85	E
- RICE CASSEROLE	95	E
- SESAME	96	E
- SICILIAN	92	G
- TIMBALES	100	G
- WILD RICE	93	B
BRUSSELS SPROUTS		
- SAUCY	88	A
- TOLERABLE	134	W
CABBAGE		
- FRIED	95	G
- RED	91	E
CARROTS		
- GRAPES, GLAZED	150	W
- L'ORANGE	153	W
- NIFTY	143	W
- *ORANGE SESAME	87	T
- PATCH	84	A
- WITH ARTICHOKES	83	A
CAULIFLOWER, CURRIED	96	G
CELERY SAUTÉ	75	A
CHILI, BARBER'S BEST	76	A
CHILIES RELLENOS	132	W
CORN		
- DEVILED	84	E
- SOUFFLÉ	80	E
*DILLED	86	T
FRUIT		
- BANANAS, BAKED	93	G
- CURRIED, HOT	96	E
GREENS, YEAR ROUND	98	E
*MEDITERRANEAN, BAKED	84	T
MUSHROOMS		
- AU GRATIN	87	A
- FESTIVE	88	E
ONIONS		
- BOOZY	144	W
- BROCCOLI, STUFFED	106	G
- CHEESE, MARINATED	105	G
- PICKLED	101	E
PARSNIPS, PERFECT	108	G

PEAS
- CASSEROLE   83 E
- COLD DILLED   144 W

PEPPERS
- JULIENNE   128 A
- PERFECT   85 A

POTATOES
- ALMONDINE, MASHED   90 E
- BUTTER-BAKED   139 W
- CREAMY, WHIPPED   81 E
- CRISPY OVEN-BAKED   78 A
- DRESSED UP SPUDS   79 A
- ELSIE'S   87 E
- FLUFFY BAKED   97 G
- GARLIC HERBED   77 A
- HASH BROWNS   95 E
- LATKES   107 G
- OVEN-BAKED FRIES   79 A
- ROASTED, HERBS   77 A
- ROSTI   98 G
- SKINS   118 W
- SWEET
  - IN ORANGE   138 W
  - SUPREME   94 E
  - YAMMY APPLE   146 W
- SWISS   78 A
- SCALLOPED
  - CHEESY   82 E
  - GRUYÈRE   89 T
  - *LIGHTEN-UP   88 T

"RATATOOEE"   74 A

RICE
- BROWN & WILD   91 T
- CASSEROLE   105 B
- CHICKEN FRIED   98 B
- COCONUT   90 T
- LEMON   80 A
- MEXICAN   93 W
- *ORANGE   146 T
- OVEN-BAKED   111 G
- PILAF   92 E
- RISOTTO   82 A

RICE CONTINUED
- SAVOURY   93 E
- WILD
  - ARTICHOKES   154 W
  - BROCCOLI   93 B
  - BUFFET   110 G
  - CASSEROLE   147 W
  - WITH MUSHROOMS   109 G

SPINACH
- EPINARDS, EH?   101 G
- POPEYE'S SOUFFLE   85 E
- TIMBALES   100 G

SQUASH
- ACORN, CHEESY   151 W
- SPAGHETTI PRIMAVERA 102 G
- SPAGHETTI, SPICY   86 A

TOMATOES
- ARTICHOKE CASSEROLE 133 W
- CHEESE BAKE   135 W
- DILL & PARMESAN   99 G
- FLORENTINE   140 W
- GREEN, FRIED   91 A
- GREEN TOMATO   97 A
    MINCEMEAT
- *ZUCCHINI STUFFED   85 T

TURNIPS
- 'N' APPLES   86 E
- PUFF   97 E

VIVA VEGGIES   90 G

ZUCCHINI
- CASSEROLE   99 E
- CHEESE FRIED   152 W
- CHEESE PIE   137 W
- ITALIAN   112 G

Order the Best of Bridge Cookbooks today!
Call our 24-hour toll-free number
1-800-883-4674
or order by using this form.

Please send:

_____ COPIES OF "THE BEST OF THE BEST and MORE" — $24.95 ($18.95 US)

_____ COPIES OF "THAT'S TRUMP" — $19.95 ($14.95 US)

_____ COPIES OF "ACES" — $19.95 ($14.95 US)

_____ COPIES OF "GRAND SLAM" — $19.95 ($14.95 US)

_____ COPIES OF "WINNERS" — $19.95 ($14.95 US)

_____ COPIES OF "ENJOY!" — $19.95 ($14.95 US)

_____ COPIES OF "THE BEST OF BRIDGE" — $19.95 ($14.95 US)

_____ Plus $6.00 for first copy postage and handling,
plus $1.00 for each additional copy Canada & US

_____ $15.00 U.S.D. postage and handling for International orders,
plus $1.00 for each additional copy

_____ Add G.S.T. (Canada only). Prices subject to change.

$ _____ is enclosed

NAME: _____

ADDRESS: _____

CITY: _____

PROV./STATE _____ POSTAL/ZIP CODE _____

Charge to ☐ VISA ☐ MASTERCARD ☐ CHEQUE

Account Number: ☐☐☐☐☐☐☐☐☐☐☐☐☐☐☐☐

Expiry Date: ☐☐☐☐

Telephone (in case we have a question about your order): _____

Ship to:

NAME: _____

ADDRESS: _____

CITY: _____

PROV./STATE _____ POSTAL/ZIP CODE _____

The Best of Bridge Publishing Ltd.

6037-6th Street S.E. • Calgary, AB • T2H 1L8 • Tel: (403) 252-0119 • Fax: (403) 252-0206
E-Mail: order@bestofbridge.com • Website: www.bestofbridge.com

The Best of Bridge Cookbook series
over 3,000,000 sold

The Best of Bridge   (The Red Book!)
Full of family favorites: "Herb Bread", "Sweet and Sour Ribs", "Rene's Sandwich Loaf", "Saturday Night Special" and "Icebox Pudding". Best known for an outstanding selection of Christmas baking.

Enjoy!   (The Yellow Book!)
Features a cross section of recipes with a strong focus on appetizers and vegetable dishes. Signature recipes include: "Ham 'N' Cheese Ball", "Fergosa", "Red Cabbage" and "Lemon Pudding". People buy this book just for the "Christmas Morning Wifesaver" recipe!

Winners   (The Green Book!)
Everything from appealing appetizers to delicious desserts. Try "Jalapeño Pepper Jelly", "Chicken Atlanta" and "Pasta Pot". "Spiked Apple Betty" and "Irish Coffee Cream Pie" will be sure-fire hits with your company!

Grand Slam   (The Black Book!)
You'll find a list of menu suggestions for all occasions. Most requested recipes include: "Bomb Shelter Croustades", "Cocktail Spread", "How Cheesy Do You Want It?" and "Teriyaki Salmon Steaks". Serve "Unattended Roast Beef" and "French Lemon Pie" — Entertaining Made Easy!

Aces   (The Blue Book!)
As always, simple recipes with gourmet results! Rave notices for "Peachy Cheese Dip", "Bruschetta", "Major Grey's Meat Loaf" and "Sticky Baked Chicken." "Sour Cream Apple Cake" and "Blueberry Buckle" are kids (big and small!) favorites. Finally — a combined index for the Best of Bridge Series!

That's Trump   (The Dark Green Book!)
Delicious fat-reduced recipes like "Hearty Tortellini Soup" and "Apple Phyllo Crisps". "Must trys" are: "Muffuletta", "Pork Loin Roast with Apple Topping", "Skor Bar Cookies" and "Easier than Apple Pie". Look for a combined index for all the Best of Bridge Cookbooks.

The Best of the Best and More   (The BIG Book!)
Over 300 pages, this latest collection brings together many old favorites and more than 70 new ones. The familiar hand-lettered format features 20 color photographs and all new jokes! Still delicious, still familiar ingredients, always "simple recipes with gourmet results".